CUT
&
DRY

Published in 2021 by
Laurence King Publishing Ltd
361–373 City Road
London EC1V 1LR
United Kingdom
email: enquiries@laurenceking.com
www.laurenceking.com

A catalogue record for this book is available
from the British Library

ISBN: 9781786278890

Photography: Ida Riveros
Design: Charlie Smith Design
Cover: Alex Coco
Commissioning Editor: Zara Larcombe

Printed in China

Laurence King Publishing is committed to
ethical and sustainable production. We are
proud participants in The Book Chain Project
Bookchainproject.com

BOOK
CHAIN
PROJECT

CUT & DRY

The Modern Guide to Dried Flowers from Growing to Styling

CAROLYN DUNSTER

Laurence King Publishing

CONTENTS

THE BEST PLANTS FOR DRYING

GROW YOUR OWN

DRYING METHODS

STYLING

PROJECTS TO TRY YOURSELF

Timeless Beauty:
A New Look at Dried Flowers

I have been obsessed with flowers for as long as I can remember. My earliest memories from childhood revolve around flowers – I loved being outside, and filling jam jars with snippings from my parents' garden was one of my favourite pastimes. Even then, however, it bothered me that once picked their beauty was fleeting, so I learned how to press and dry flowers to make them last.

Drying flowers is an ancient art that has been practised for millennia, but in recent history the pastime has rather fallen out of favour. The increased choice and year-round availability of fresh cut flowers, combined with our constant search for something new and different, put dried flowers in the shade, but recently I've been happy to see that a growing band of eco-aware artisan florists have started using them again in their work. As the movement for locally grown, seasonal flowers surges ahead, dried flowers are the answer to filling the gaps between the seasons, and they can be reused to stretch the life of event and installation flowers, reducing waste and increasing sustainability in the cut-flower industry.

It's been proven that contact with nature is essential to our daily well-being, and if we are living and working in cities this can be tricky. Assembling a few dried blooms and berries, some foraged twigs and seed heads to create changeable seasonal displays is an inexpensive way of bringing a little bit of the natural world into our homes with no added maintenance issues. Dried material does not have to mean dull and dusty, and it is fast shedding its old-fashioned connotations.

The idea for this book came about when I was on holiday on the Greek island of Tinos. For the first time in my life I saw swathes of statice (*Limonium sinuatum*) growing in the wild. It's a flower that I had always studiously avoided, even though it's known for its fantastic drying tendency. I never liked its stiff, rigid stems, which refuse to twist and turn like other home-grown blooms, or the feel of its desiccated papery florets, but seeing it growing in its natural habitat made me think again. I liked the way its bright colours held out against the vivid blue of the sea and sky and the wavy pattern that its winged leafless stems make when they grow densely together.

I also noticed how the flowers were celebrated. On an island where any available planting space is turned over to cultivating fruits and vegetables, rather than growing flowers, the wild statice had been picked and used in taverna table arrangements and for door wreaths. There were flowers everywhere that had been cut and dried – no water required – and they would last all season as a beautiful welcoming gesture.

Back home I decided to grow some statice myself; its botanical name, *Limonium*, comes from the Greek word *leimon*, meaning salt meadow, which is where it grows freely, and in a tiny urban garden miles away from the sea it took a while to get going, but I did manage to harvest a few stems. The key for me is mixing them with other flowers, seed heads and grasses that I have dried myself, and I hope the following pages demonstrate that there's nothing difficult or complicated about doing this – it's a new old way of appreciating flowers in all their glorious stages of life.

Plant names

In most cases I have used the common name of plants and flowers, followed by the botanical or Latin name. The universal classification of plants was set up by the Swedish botanist Carl Linnaeus in 1735 and is still in practice today as the correct means for plant identification across the horticultural world. When I trained as a garden designer, learning our 'plant idents' by rote was an important part of the course and we were tested on them weekly. I thought I would never keep them in my head, but the more I work with flowers and plants the more the names stick. It's like learning a whole new exciting language.

Left Dried statice flowers, a wonderful reminder of wild Greek meadows.

Opposite
Top left Stems of pink bistort provide good ground cover, with abundant flowers for cutting and drying.

Top right Astrantia and columbine – two cottage garden favourites that flower profusely.

Bottom My tiny city garden is filled with flowers that I grow for drying.

The Best Plants for Drying

If you have a garden, an allotment or even a few balcony pots you will already have something growing that is suitable for drying. Any plant material will dry out under the right conditions, although certain plants retain their colour, form and texture better than others. Experimentation is the key to successful drying.

Choosing Your Plant Material

Drying plants and flowers is a way to extend their natural lifespan. By removing the moisture from their different component parts – petals, leaves, stalks – it is possible to keep them in a state of semi-permanence. This lets us look at them in a new light and handle them differently as they become brittle and fragile, while still appreciating their beauty.

As a rule of thumb, any drought-tolerant plant grown in the garden should dry out successfully. The lists of plants presented in this chapter include everything that I have tried and tested for drying with successful results. Information about growing different plant materials yourself – if this is an option – is provided in the next chapter. Otherwise, knowing when and where to look for natural pickings also gives you opportunities to experiment – you can gather pretty fallen leaves from pavements in the autumn or forage for seed heads in the wild. Buying bunches of fresh flowers from a florist or supermarket, or picking out the right varieties from regular flower subscription services or when you're given a bouquet as a gift, can also be a hassle-free way to build up your dried flower collection.

To avoid the drying process altogether, you can also buy dried flowers directly from specialist suppliers. These can provide a good starting point, although the ranges are usually limited, and they never look quite as good as anything you have dried yourself.

I've divided everything into groups according to type, and indicated the best drying or preservation method for each plant. For notes on each one, see 'Drying Methods' (pages 100–123). If you take a few suggestions from each section, you will soon amass a good variety of materials to create your own long-lasting displays and arrangements. Bear in mind that my recommendations are by no means exhaustive. Drying flowers is not an exact science. It doesn't have to cost a lot of money or take up a lot of time, so play around with a few flowers and leaves, some mosses and berries. The more you experiment, the more you will get a feel for what will dry out well, and you may get a few lovely surprises on the way.

Opposite
Top left The delicate teardrop heads of quaking grass, paired with pink Oxford cranesbill flowers.
Top right An ornamental onion growing through a large clump of lemon balm.
Bottom left A bright blue love-in-a-mist flower will mature into a wonderful seed head.
Bottom right Lime-green stems of hare's ear and mountain cranesbill.

FLOWERS

Everyone has a favourite flower. It could be a bloom from childhood that links you to a particular time or place, one that holds significance because of a special occasion, or simply a variety that you love because you find it easy to grow. This may be the best place to start your own drying experiments and to watch as the textures and colours slowly change in front of your eyes.

In my own garden I grow the usual suspects for drying: strawflowers (*Xerochrysum*), statice (*Limonium*) and mophead hydrangeas (*Hydrangea macrophylla*). I know these plants dry out well, but I also like to experiment. A glut of self-seeded early-flowering spurges (*Euphorbia*) threatened to take over my tiny space and needed thinning out. Instead of putting them on the compost heap, I hung them up to dry and the results were fantastic, their acid-green bracts remaining intact and zingy. Never be afraid to try things out and see what happens; it is all part of the fun.

Some flower heads, such as hydrangeas, change colour as they dry; the pigments take on a mottled appearance and they look all the better for it. Red, purple, mauve and blue flowers will keep their original colour longest, but in time you should learn to embrace the colour brown – all dried material will eventually fade, but preserved shapes and forms provide everlasting keepsakes of flowers from special occasions. The next pages will introduce you to flowers that can be dried particularly successfully.

Strawflower (*Xerochrysum*)

Available in a variety of colours, from pink and pale peach through to dark crimson and claret. Grow from seed or as plug plants for an annual harvest. Rapid results from air- and heat-source drying.

Statice (*Limonium*)

Its stiff, desiccated appearance is not to everyone's taste. Grow as an annual from seed or buy it from a florist, freshly cut or pre-dried. Air-dries almost instantly when laid flat.

Cockscomb (*Celosia*)

An annual to grow from seed or purchase in season from your local florist. It bears unusual and exotic-looking plume-like flower heads that come in a range of reds, pinks and golds. Air-dry.

Strawflower

Statice

Cockscomb

Love-Lies-Bleeding (*Amaranthus caudatus*)
Deep crimson annual flowers that are easy to grow from seed. Their pendulous tufted heads dry to a dramatically darker shade. Air-dry.

Pot Marigold (*Calendula*)
Annual flowers to grow from seed with bright orange heads that keep their colour well when dried and look good in mixed arrangements. Air-dry.

Scabious (*Scabiosa*)

Also known as the pincushion flower, the many different varieties of scabious all make great dried flowers. The tight, compact heads retain their shape perfectly and can be picked at different stages of flowering for an interesting mix. Grow from seed as pretty cottage garden annuals in a range of pale pastel colours, or forage for its close relation field scabious (*Knautia arvensis*) in the wild. Air-dry all types.

Valerian (*Valeriana officinalis*)

You'll find this in the wild. It's easy to spot because of its height: valerian will grow up to 1.5 metres (5 feet) tall. It's the perfect plant for growing at the back of a narrow border or along a wall or fence. Its dense clusters of tiny star-shaped flowers start off white but often take on a pink tinge; there is also a pink variety with flowers that deepen to red. Cut the long stems at their base for air-drying.

Valerian

Scabious

Yarrow (*Achillea*)

You can gather stems of yellow common yarrow in the wild or grow it yourself from seed or plugs. As they dry the flower heads mellow, losing their brassy tones. If the yellow is not to your taste, you'll find garden varieties in more subtle hues. Air-dry.

Safflower (*Carthamus tinctorius*)

Cultivated commercially as a cheap alternative to saffron. These annual flowers have deep orange-red thistle-like heads that dry out to perfection. Easy to grow yourself from seed and air-dry, but you'll also find it from any dried flower supplier.

Billy Buttons (*Craspedia*)

Half-hardy annual flowers to grow from seed or buy as seasonal cut flowers. Delicate yellow pom-pom heads sit atop erect straight stems for simple, minimal displays. Vase-dry or air-dry.

Yarrow

Safflower

Billy
Buttons

Bistort (*Persicaria bistorta*)

All types of bistort dry out well. You'll see its dark pink spiky flowers growing like a weed in the countryside, and even through cracks in city pavements. The domestic perennial types are a little more refined and well worth growing as rapid foliage ground cover with flowers appearing in mid-summer to harvest and air-dry.

Astrantia (*Astrantia*)

A personal favourite perennial for growing and drying. My garden is full of it as it pops up all over the place, self-seeding every year from just a couple of original plants. The really dark varieties, such as 'Ruby Cloud' and 'Ruby Wedding', dry out best. Air-dry.

Fiddleneck (*Phacelia tanacetifolia*)

A wonderful annual flower with bell-shaped lavender heads to grow from seed as part of a wildflower scheme. Grown in succession, it provides great ground cover and easy pickings for regular drying. Air-dry.

Astrantia

Bistort

Fiddleneck

Sea Lavender (*Limonium latifolium*)

Similar in texture to statice but grows as a garden perennial; it is also found in the wild near water, where it is known as marsh rosemary. Its smaller flowers on bushier stems make it a more attractive alternative to traditional statice. Vase-dry.

Clover (*Trifolium*)

Pick in the wild or grow it yourself as a perennial flower. Clover makes a fabulous alternative lawn that attracts bees and other pollinators. Pick it in full flower: the tufted pink pom-pom heads hold their shape well. Air-dry.

Acroclinium (*Helipterum roseum*)

Familiar as a dried flower with delicate pink and white heads on wispy stems. Grow it from seed as an annual flower and air-dry, or purchase direct from a dried flower supplier.

Freesia (*Freesia*)

I like to buy these in early spring as fresh flowers specifically for their wonderful scent: display half the bunch in a vase and press the rest between sheets of blotting paper. They will lose their perfume but retain their delicate form and colour.

Sea Lavender

Clover

Acroclinium

Freesia

Larkspur (*Delphinium*)
An annual flowering plant that is easy to grow yourself. Its tall, dense flower spikes dry out beautifully on long stems. Choose the blue or purple varieties for best results. Air-dry.

Sea Holly (*Eryngium*)
An unusual blue-grey flowering perennial with sculptural thistle-shaped heads that dry brilliantly and keep their colour. Grow in your garden or source from a flower shop for air-drying.

Larkspur

Sea Holly

Columbine

Columbine (*Aquilegia*)

There are over 60 different species of this spring-flowering perennial. Choose a colour you love and let it spread itself around your garden, self-seeding over time so you can cut and air-dry with abandon.

Spurge (*Euphorbia*)

Different types of euphorbia are in flower year-round. They are well-loved garden perennials that spread prolifically. Though you might not choose to cultivate them specifically for cutting and drying, they make an unusual dried flower and look good massed together in a huge bunch. Air-dry.

Cornflower (*Centaurea montana*)

A familiar cottage garden perennial, with blue and purple varieties that hold their colour well when dried. Mix with wild annual cornflowers found in fields and meadows, which grow easily from seed in a domestic setting. Air-dry.

Cornflower

Spurge

Baby's Breath

Baby's Breath (*Gypsophila*)
The leader of the dried flower fashion pack, its tiny white florets hold their shape beautifully. Purchase in large bunches for creating botanical clouds and other airy, ethereal arrangements. Air-dry or vase-dry.

Honeywort (*Cerinthe*)
A hardy annual, easy to grow from seed and popular with cut-flower growers. Once picked and dried, its tiny purple hanging bells retain their colour and shape well. Air-dry.

Honeywort

Hare's Ear (*Bupleurum rotundifolium*)
The tiny green-yellow florets of this annual flowering plant will be familiar as a filler from shop-bought flower arrangements. Grow it yourself from seed or buy bunches from your florist for immediate air-drying.

Lady's Mantle (*Alchemilla mollis*)
This early-flowering perennial spreads quickly around the garden. Its fluffy lime-green flowers sit on mounds of lovely rosette-shaped leaves. Pick in full flower for air-drying and you will be rewarded with a second flush of flowers later in the summer.

Hare's Ear

Lady's Mantle

False Goat's Beard

False Goat's Beard *(Astilbe)*

A wonderful perennial plant to grow from seed or as a plug. As its common name suggests, it produces large, fluffy beard-shaped plumes in a range of hues from cream to deep burgundy, cerise and crimson on coloured stems that stiffen up as the moisture is drawn out. Air-dry.

Brook Thistle *(Cirsium rivulare)*

In early summer, deep claret-coloured thistles appear in clusters on the tall, rigid stems of this dramatic biennial plant. Cut it from its base for a fantastic dried display. Air-dry.

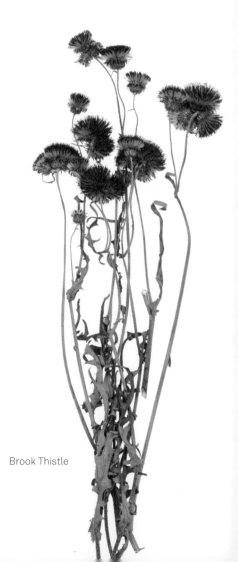

Brook Thistle

Waxflower (*Chamelaucium*)
This Australian native is not easy to grow in the northern hemisphere, but it is often included as a filler flower in shop-bought bouquets because it is so long-lasting. Buy it year-round and vase- or air-dry.

Rose (*Rosa*)

For drying purposes I recommend buying wraps of supermarket roses, unless you have so many growing in your garden that you are happy to sacrifice them before they come into full flower. For best results, dry roses on the stem just as the buds are opening. The heads of garden-grown roses in full bloom can be dried in sand or over a heat source. Alternatively, collect petals as they drop from the flower head to make your own confetti.

Peony (*Paeonia*)

The flowering season for peonies is all too brief, so I prefer not to pick them from my garden but rather to purchase bunches of blooms, particularly the pink and claret colours, from local growers at the farmers' market. Stand in them water and allow the tight, fat buds to come into early flower before drying. Air-dry or dry in sand.

Rose

Peony

Mophead Hydrangea
(*Hydrangea macrophylla*)

An invaluable perennial for lovers of dried flowers. Blue hydrangeas will keep their colour if you grow them in acidic compost. Their large heads fade and mottle beautifully as they dry out on the stem; pick them as they turn papery and they will last for ages. Shop-bought hydrangeas will dry easily in a vase.

HERBS

Broadly speaking, herbs are distinct from flowers because of their particular culinary and medicinal properties. Herb gardens or apothecary gardens were originally planted in medieval times and cultivated for healing purposes. Both fresh and dried herbs were used for making tisanes, tinctures and pastes to treat all manner of ailments.

Today, herbs are more commonly used in cooking than in medicine, but they are still win-win plants to grow yourself, being both useful and decorative. String up your drying herbs in the kitchen – they won't take up much space and will make a beautiful display, as well as adding extra flavour to your food.

- The yellow buttons of flowering cotton lavender (*Santolina chamaecyparissus*) **(1)** were traditionally used in the preparation of herbal remedies. Today they are more commonly used as a moth repellent.

- Thyme (*Thymus vulgaris*) **(2, 4)** and sage (*Salvia officinalis*) thrive well in troughs and pots. Cut bushy, woody stems for the best dried results.

- Rosemary (*Salvia rosmarinus*) **(3)** and bay (*Laurus nobilis*) **(5)** require space to grow outside if you want them to flower, but if you can get your hands on a few fresh sprigs, along with their tiny flowers, they are a lovely addition to your drying display.

- Both lavender (*Lavandula*) **(6)** and chamomile (*Chamaemelum nobile*) **(7)** flowers dry attractively. Use the tiny chamomile heads for tisanes and the lavender (sparingly) to flavour sweet treats.

- Chives (*Allium schoenoprasum*) **(8)** are a member of the onion family. Their delicate pink flower heads stay intact when dry and are totally edible along with their stems.

- The bright blue flowers of borage (*Borago officinalis*) **(9)** close up slightly as they dry, but make a pretty pop of colour in a bunch of drying herbs, and can be used for flavouring cocktails and soft drinks.

- Marjoram (*Origanum majorana*) and oregano (*Origanum vulgare*), along with peppermint (*Mentha x piperita*), produce lovely flower heads (if allowed) that dry out beautifully.

- Dill (*Anethum graveolens*) and fennel (*Foeniculum vulgare*) produce umbel-shaped yellow flowers that hold their structure really well when dry.

FOLIAGE AND FERNS

The leaves of plants and trees have their own intrinsic beauty. Discover a breathtaking array of colours, patterns, shapes and textures by drying and preserving different types of foliage. They will provide material for creating stunning displays, with or without added flowers.

Trees fulfil a wide range of ecological functions and are vital to the health of our planet and our personal well-being. Without them, human survival would be at risk. We tend to take them for granted, however, and as often as not we don't really notice the trees and their leaves that are the background to our lives. By collecting and preserving different types of foliage from trees, shrubs and ferns, whether evergreen or deciduous, we make them the focus of our attention.

You can pick up leaves from city parks, country woods or suburban streets, but if you have space I would urge you to grow at least one tree. Choose a variety with year-round interest, such as a white-stemmed Himalayan birch (*Betula utilis* var. *jacquemontii*), with its beautiful peeling bark (see page 59), bright green foliage in spring and summer, and pendulous catkins in winter that make fabulous dried displays.

Green Leaves

Most green leaves can be picked for drying at any point during the growing season, but fresh young, bushy growth will stay verdant for longer in its dried state than older woody stems.

Ruscus (*Ruscus*)

With its delicate dark green leaves, ruscus is commonly found in fresh flower arrangements because it lasts for ages, drying out slowly. Buy a single bushy bunch and split the stems before hanging up to air-dry.

Shepherd's Purse (*Capsella bursa-pastoris*)

The tiny heart-shaped leaves of this perennial appear in late spring. You will find it growing in the wild. Pick the leaves from the base of the plant and they will retain their shape and colour as they air-dry.

Box (*Buxus*), Sweet Box (*Sarcococca*) and Yew (*Taxus*)

These evergreen garden shrubs require regular clipping to keep their shape. Save extra-long cuttings and air-dry.

Conifers

Conifer foliage lasts for ages, retaining its colour and scent. It is good for foliage-heavy arrangements such as wreaths and garlands. Forage for or purchase different varieties of evergreen pine and fir and mix them together. Vase-dry.

Yew

Shepherd's Purse

Ruscus

Box

Silver Leaves

Silver/grey foliage dries out particularly well and keeps its true colour for a long time. Many Mediterranean plants have silvery leaves – they thrive in dry conditions, absorb little moisture and therefore dry very quickly.

Cardoon (*Cynara cardunculus*)

Look out for the oversized silvery leaves and harvest at the same time as the seed heads. Air-dry.

Cotton Lavender (*Santolina*), Daisy Bush (*Brachyglottis*) and Germander (*Teucrium fruticans*)

These garden plants are all easy to grow and bear differently shaped silver/grey leaves for picking and air-drying; discard any flowers.

Senecio (*Senecio cineraria* 'Silver Dust')

If you have space for only one foliage plant, choose senecio, which can be grown indoors or outdoors. The leaves look as if they have been cut out with a stencil; air-dry or press them flat to appreciate the lovely shapes fully.

Eucalyptus (*Eucalyptus*)

Eucalyptus foliage is available in different varieties: buy either the long, thin-tipped leaves or the round, twisted type in bunches from a florist. Pleasingly, it retains its aromatic scent as it dries. Air-dry or vase-dry.

Cardoon

Daisy Bush

Senecio

Eucalyptus

Coloured Leaves

As autumn approaches and the green chlorophyll breaks down in the leaves of deciduous trees and shrubs, they change colour. This is the time of year to forage or pick leaves in brilliant shades of gold, russet, cerise and crimson. Choose an array of contrasting shapes and colours for pressing and preserving to make your own leaf mandala.

Red Barberry (*Berberis thunbergii*)

This ornamental shrub has oval-shaped, cerise-coloured leaves that fade to a dark claret as they air-dry.

Ginkgo (*Ginkgo biloba*), Japanese Maple (*Acer palmatum*), Mountain Ash or Rowan (*Sorbus*) and Snowy Mespilus (*Amelanchier*)

Leaves from these ornamental trees keep their colours and shapes when pressed flat.

Copper Beech (*Fagus sylvatica* f. *purpurea*) and Oak (*Quercus*)

Bunches of beautiful bronze leaves from these trees will keep their colour best if preserved in a glycerine solution.

Oak, red barberry, snowy mespilus and copper beech

Copper Beech

Oak

Ferns

For classification purposes, ferns fall into their own distinct plant group. They are one of the earth's earliest known plants, and thrive by reproducing through spores, bearing no flowers or fruit.

Polystichum (*Polystichum*), Asplenium (*Asplenium*) and Shuttlecock Fern (*Matteuccia*)

If you have any damp, shady spots in your garden, fill them with ferns. These varieties will give you many different shapes for air-drying.

Boston Fern (*Nephrolepis exaltata*), Maidenhair Fern (*Adiantum*) and Emerald Fern (*Asparagus densiflorus*)

These varieties grow best indoors. Pick single fronds for pressing or cut a small group and air-dry; watch them curl gently as they do so.

Asparagus Fern (*Asparagus setaceus*)

Despite its name, this is not strictly speaking a fern. Its delicate, feathery leaves can be bought in bunches from florists for vase-drying to create wonderful, airy green displays, and they hold up really well to spray-painting in shimmering colours.

Asparagus fern, polystichum and bracken

Bracken (*Pteridium*)

Forage for these large, coarse ferns in the autumn as their colour is fading and they are turning brown. Each frond is made up of tiny individual leaves. They air-dry well and look good gilded or gently spray-painted.

GRASSES

Defined and categorized by their long, slender leaves, grasses make up their own distinct family group within the plant kingdom, and there are hundreds to choose from. They are incredibly successful colonizers, with a natural habitat of wide open spaces: think of the African savannah or the pampas plains of South America, where grasses are the main type of vegetation.

You'll also see grasses growing in nature reserves and protected areas of natural beauty, but they will settle in anywhere they get the chance. If you decide to grow them in your own garden, make sure you choose a variety that isn't going to take over. Home-grown grasses are generally low maintenance and look good in any planting combination. You can find a grass for nearly any situation – just check the information on the label. Because they have shallow root systems, grasses grow well in outdoor containers; this also prevents them from spreading too far and makes them easy to harvest for drying.

If you're growing your own grasses (see pages 94–95), the following are good for small pots or tight spaces: quaking grass, blue fescue, sedge, Japanese forest grass, snow-white wood-rush and northern sea oats (pages 46–47). For large pots and open spaces, try bunny's tail grass, bamboo, silver grass, pheasant grass, pampas grass, switch grass or cloud grass, and foxtail millet (pages 48–51).

You can forage in the wild for moor grass, plantain grass, Persian rye grass, tufted hair grass, flowering rye grass and reed grass (pages 52–53).

Some grasses are deciduous and produce beautiful flowering spikelets; others are evergreen and retain their colour and form year-round. They're all incredibly tactile and gently soothing as they rustle in a breeze, making them the ultimate feel-good plants.

Both the foliage and flowers of grasses make beautiful dried material. Here are some points to bear in mind:

- All grasses can be dried on the stem (see page 109).
- Cut flowering stems when they feel dry to the touch, normally in autumn or early winter. They will have lost all their moisture naturally and require no further treatment.
- Evergreen foliage can be cut at any time and will dry out gradually once it's been arranged.
- Styling is easy – just keep it simple with no other flowers or added colour for soft subtle arrangements.
- Arrange extra-tall feathery plumes in a narrow container to create a dramatic focal point.
- Place three bunches of contrasting pendulous grasses in a shallow, wide-necked vase to bring a minimally decorated room to life.

Quaking Grass (*Briza media*)

Extremely easy semi-evergreen grass to grow from seed (see pages 94–95). Leave some of the tiny teardrop heads to self-seed, and it will reliably come back year after year.

Blue Fescue (*Festuca glauca*)

An unusually coloured blue-tinged grass that looks fantastic year-round and produces extra-tall feathery flowers for a short period in the summer. Harvest both flowers and foliage.

Sedge (*Carex*)

Grows in a neat hummock shape and will sit attractively in a shallow pot, with its thin, reed-like leaves dripping over the sides. Classed as an evergreen, it comes in a range of colours from gold to grey. The flower heads gradually change colour as they dry in a vase.

Quaking Grass

Blue Fescue

Sedge

Japanese Forest Grass (*Hakonechloa*)

Fine, light sprays of lime-green flowers appear on the cascading hummocks of this lovely deciduous grass throughout the summer. The flowers and foliage fade to a golden russet for cutting in the autumn.

Snow-White Wood-Rush (*Luzula nivea*)

The best grass for a really small pot, it will keep its hairy green leaves year-round and produces sprays of delicate white flowers from early spring, which dry to brown for harvesting.

Northern Sea Oats (*Chasmanthium latifolium*)

This graceful perennial grass starts off with bright green heads that look like miniature ears of wheat. As they dry, they turn a lovely golden brown.

Snow-White
Wood-Rush

Japanese Forest Grass

Northern Sea Oats

Bunny's Tail Grass (*Lagurus ovatus*)
Grow these gorgeous fluffy tufts from seed
or as plug plants at the front of a border. It
flowers for several months to provide constant
material for picking and drying.

Bamboo (*Phyllostachys*)
Needs careful consideration, because it
can be very invasive and is not suitable for
small gardens unless you grow it in a pot or
otherwise restrict its roots. The delicate green
leaves and varieties with black or gold canes
make fantastic dried material, however.

Silver Grass (*Miscanthus*)
For drama and structure outdoors, this is
one of the best grasses to grow. It will reach
2.5 metres (about 8 feet), and its lovely fluffy
heads are all you need to create a stand-out
dried arrangement. Harvest them gradually
throughout the autumn and winter and raze
the whole plant to the ground when all the
tufts have been picked.

Bunny's Tail Grass

Silver Grass

Bamboo

Pampas Grass

Pheasant Grass

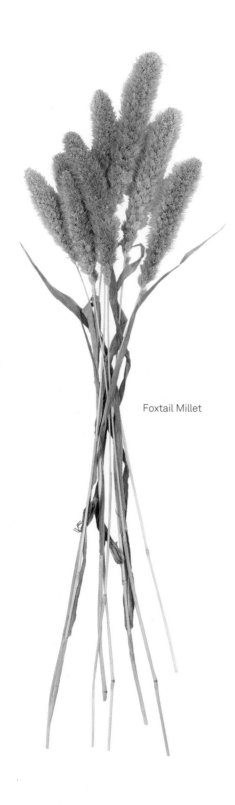

Foxtail Millet

Pampas Grass (*Cortaderia*)

A native plant of South America, this grass is much maligned for its invasive tendencies, but for drying purposes its tall, feathery plumes are invaluable. Try growing the dwarf compact variety 'Pumila', or source it pre-dried online from a specialist supplier if you don't have space.

Pheasant Grass (*Stipa arundinacea*)

Forms fountain-like clumps with foliage that starts off green but gradually turns to a streaky combination of reds, yellows and oranges. It should be picked at this stage to bring indoors.

Foxtail Millet (*Setaria*)

A half-hardy annual grass to grow from seed in a mixed border or large pot, with attractive tufted panicles (flower clusters) to harvest and keep.

Switch Grass or Cloud Grass (*Panicum virgatum*)

A North American prairie grass with upright leaves. It bears tiny spikelet flowers that look fantastic massed together when dry. It is a deciduous grass that can be razed to the ground after harvesting.

Switch Grass or Cloud Grass

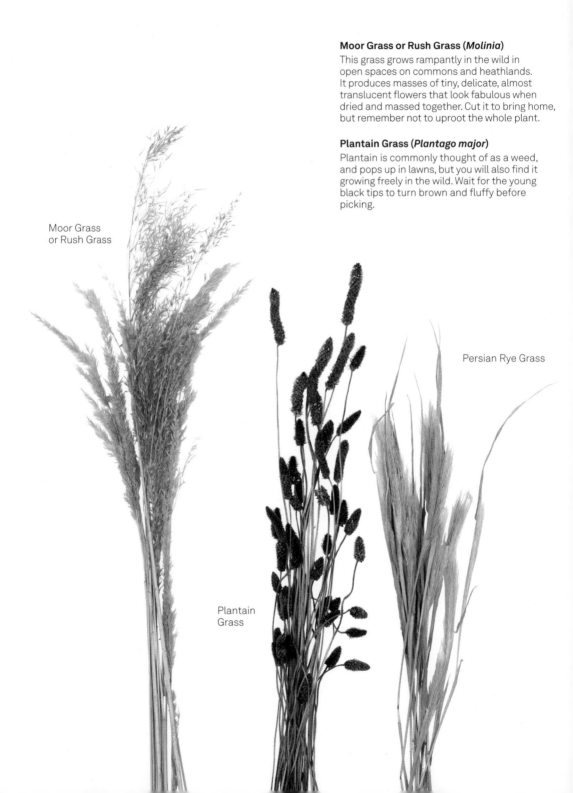

Moor Grass or Rush Grass (*Molinia*)

This grass grows rampantly in the wild in open spaces on commons and heathlands. It produces masses of tiny, delicate, almost translucent flowers that look fabulous when dried and massed together. Cut it to bring home, but remember not to uproot the whole plant.

Plantain Grass (*Plantago major*)

Plantain is commonly thought of as a weed, and pops up in lawns, but you will also find it growing freely in the wild. Wait for the young black tips to turn brown and fluffy before picking.

Moor Grass
or Rush Grass

Persian Rye Grass

Plantain
Grass

Persian Rye Grass (*Lolium persicum*)

This is an annual grass with flowering heads that resemble wheat. You will see it growing everywhere, because it is very invasive. Pick as the heads start to yellow.

Tufted Hair Grass (*Deschampsia*)

A beautiful light, feathery grass with thread-like leaves. The delicate panicles turn from green to gold during its growing season. Harvest in abundance for a gorgeous indoor display.

Flowering Rye Grass (*Lolium*)

You will spot this all over the place. It is a perennial grass that is commonly grown in the northern hemisphere as part of a lawn mix. Left to its own devices it will grow to about 50 centimetres (20 inches) and flower in the summer. Pick it wherever you see it growing, and leave it to dry.

Reed Grass or Canary Grass (*Phalaris*)

You will find this grass growing by streams and ponds. Its attractive purple-tinged flower spikelets dry beautifully.

Tufted Hair Grass

Flowering Rye Grass

Reed Grass or Canary Grass

MOSSES AND LICHENS

Mosses and lichens are complex and fascinating ancient life forms. They are tiny microcosms containing a living world – the antiseptic and antibacterial organisms they contain made them a viable alternative to wound dressings in the First World War. Their gorgeous velvety textures invite touch, and once dry they are a fantastic addition to natural dried arrangements.

Mosses are tiny flowerless plants that grow in dense clumps or mats. They can be found in damp and shady places, where they colonize bare ground. To encourage moss to grow in your garden, don't scrape it away but break up big pieces and replant them, making sure to keep them very moist. Alternatively, buy it from florists or online craft suppliers.

- Silver moss **(1)** comes in a range of natural colours but is also readily available in dyed shades.
- Reindeer moss **(2)** is a dry moss that won't change at all over time.
- Bun moss **(3)** can be bought in trays that look like small grassy hillocks; it dries out very slowly.
- Spanish moss **(4)**, strictly speaking, is an air plant, but you can use it in arrangements in lieu of any other moss.
- Carpet moss or flat moss **(5)** will keep its brilliant green colour forever.

Lichens are spores that grow on a host – spot them growing on trees, rocks and walls. They thrive by extracting water from the atmosphere, and you'll find them predominantly in coastal areas where there is a lot of moisture in the air. There are hundreds of different lichens in a rich colour palette from oranges, yellows and rusty browns through to all the greens. Forage for them by collecting fallen twigs and branches, or by picking up larger pieces that have come away from the host. They dry out quickly, becoming crispy to the touch. Lichen-covered twigs create a framework to support fragile dried flowers and foliage in vase arrangements. Use larger pieces to cover chicken wire in bowl arrangements.

Opposite Use dried moss and lichen to construct miniature gardens in glass vessels such as vases (see page 160). Layer moss with pebbles and twigs, and insert some small dried flower stems or seed heads into the moss so that they look as though they are growing. The moss and pebbles will support the flowers and keep them upright.

BARK, BRANCHES AND TWIGS

Cutting and drying twigs and stems from trees and collecting pieces of coloured tree bark is a lovely, simple way to bring nature indoors. Studies show that living among nature is beneficial to our health and well-being, and a single branch of unfurling leaves or tight flower buds captured and dried in that moment is all you need to inject a sense of hope and promise into your surroundings.

All trees naturally shed their bark as they grow. Their trunks expand from the inside, producing new inner layers and causing the outer layers to break off and come away. Extreme shedding can also indicate that a tree is in distress. In periods of drought, trees that thrive on a lot of water will lose large bits of bark, and you'll find them scattered across the pavements under city trees in very hot weather.

This is the time to collect workable pieces from planes (*Platanus*) and sycamores (*Acer pseudoplatanus*) – the most common city trees – to bring home. Paint them with a coat of olive oil, which will bring out their beautiful textures and colours. Use smaller pieces to tie around glass jars and vases to make your own organic-looking flower-holders, or use large pieces as a base for displaying tiny delicate stems of dried flowers, mosses and pebbles in a Japanese ikebana-inspired arrangement (see page 143).

The beautiful white bark of silver birch (*Betula pendula*) is also well worth collecting. The tough, water-resistant cardboard-like bark of birch trees has been used as a building material since prehistoric times. You can buy it in large pieces from online suppliers; it is easily bent and can be cut into any shape for all kinds of craft projects. Alternatively, forage for the papery outer layers as you see them: they fall away from the tree in delicate furling strips that you can collect from the ground and incorporate into bunches and bouquets.

In springtime you can cut smaller branches of trees just as they are coming into leaf or flower, and they will remain at this stage for weeks and even months before the newly formed buds eventually drop off. Look for the bright yellow buttons of mimosa (*Mimosa*), the pink-purple tufts of wisteria (*Wisteria*) and the silvery, furry buds of pussy willow (*Salix*). The tight, unfurling buds of chestnut trees (*Castanea*) also look fantastic. Many blossoms will dry out if you pick them before they are fully in flower. Air-dry or vase-dry.

You'll also find catkins forming on many trees, including willows, birches (*Betula*), alders (*Alnus*), hazels (*Corylus*) and hornbeams (*Carpinus*). They last for ages, but make sure to collect them before they start to produce pollen, because it makes a terrible mess inside and the catkins are too soft by then to dry successfully.

In autumn, gather coloured stems to keep for making festive decorations. Willow stems are available to buy online from basket-making supply sites. If you soak the stems, they will become pliable enough to work with; twist them into shapes for making your own wreath bases and small containers (see pages 140, 155, 158).

You can also do this with foraged stems of old man's beard (*Clematis vitalba*), Russian vine (*Fallopia baldschuanica*) and Virginia creeper (*Parthenocissus quinquefolia*). The red, orange, yellow, lime-green, purple and black stems of different dogwoods (*Cornus*) dry out beautifully and keep their colour. You can grow dogwood easily, even in a small garden, and keep the prunings when you cut it back. Remove any remaining bits of foliage and vase-dry.

Gather small sticks or dead, bushy twigs when you see them. They are really useful as natural props for your dry displays (see page 137). Because the thin, wispy stems of dried flowers are not self-supporting, they need help in order to stand upright. Cut straight lengths of dried twigs and wire them together to make a grid to use as a framework over the top of a vase to keep your flowers straight, or push a bunched ball of twiggy stems into a vase or vessel to provide support. If the stems are very dry, wet them first to make them easier to work with, but make sure they are completely dry before adding any flowers. This looks much nicer than chicken wire and doesn't need covering or disguising.

Right Willow catkins
Opposite Mimosa branches

SEED HEADS AND PODS

Seeds are the magical component of every flowering plant. Each one has the potential to guarantee the future survival of a species, and some varieties go to extraordinary and fascinating lengths to make this happen. Once pollination has taken place, seeds form as ovules inside the reproductive centre, or pistil, of the plant as it reaches the end of its flowering period.

Gardening wisdom will tell you to deadhead or remove any spent blooms at this stage in order to encourage further flowering, but if you put away the secateurs and watch what happens next, it is nothing short of miraculous. As the petals fade away, the pistil will gradually start to swell as the seeds inside develop and ripen, eventually forming a distinctive head or pod.

The varying forms and textures of harvested dried heads and pods offer a huge amount of scope to create stunning indoor displays that last for ages. Left to dry on the stem, they do the work for you – just choose the ones you like the look of. Examine them up close and study their detail, and you'll find them truly amazing.

Many seed heads and pods are every bit as beautiful and fascinating to look at as their original flowers, in some cases more so. Honesty's (*Lunaria annua*) shimmering, almost translucent seed heads are far more striking than its clusters of small purple flowers.

All flower types have developed their own unique seed dispersal mechanisms, and this dictates the structure and shape of the pod or head. Mixing them up brings depth and interest to your displays. Soft, fluffy seed heads are blown from the parent plant by the wind, scattered far and wide. Old man's beard (*Clematis vitalba*) is a good example – you'll see it growing in the wild, dramatically draping hedgerows in temporary white blankets. Gather it when you can.

Pocket-like pods have sturdier shells or casings that are vacuum-packed and will burst open when the seed is ripe, dispersing it by pure force. Opium poppies (*Papaver somniferum*) develop seed pods that are a feat of natural engineering, complete with their own built-in air vents. If you harvest the heads before they are completely empty, you will hear the tiny seeds rattling inside. Hang them upside down in a paper bag to collect the seeds for future sowing before you arrange the pods.

**Drumstick Scabious
(*Scabiosa stellata* 'Sternkugel')**

These intriguing globular seed heads are top of my list of favourites (see page 92 for instructions on how to grow them from seed). Mix with the dried flower heads of other varieties of scabious for a wonderful display.

Ornamental Onion (*Allium*)

Any member of this perennial plant family produces spectacular spherical seed heads, which make a beautiful natural alternative to Christmas baubles. Growing a few different varieties will give you a choice of sizes, but all you really need for a striking display is one huge head of *Allium cristophii*, or star of Persia.

Cow Parsley (*Anthriscus sylvestris*)

Locate a patch of this growing wild in early summer – you will recognize its white, lacy flowers – and keep an eye on it. It turns to seed quite quickly if the weather is warm. Once it starts to turn brown and feels dry to the touch, cut it and display; the tiny florets are very delicate, so handle gently.

Drumstick Scabious

Ornamental Onion

Cow Parsley

African Lily (*Agapanthus*)

A great plant for growing in pots as it likes to be in a tight space. Its striking blue and white flowers bloom from mid-summer onwards and by autumn turn into gorgeous globular heads to bring indoors.

Blue False Indigo (*Baptisia australis*)

The bright blue pea-like flowers on this easy-to-grow perennial plant form the most amazing black seed heads that rattle spectacularly like sets of maracas before dispersing.

Yarrow (*Achillea*)

Like its flowers (see page 21), yarrow seed heads dry out really well. Leave some flower heads in the garden all winter and you will be rewarded with delicate skeleton forms of the original flowers. Display the dried flowers and seed heads together.

Yarrow

Blue False Indigo

African Lily

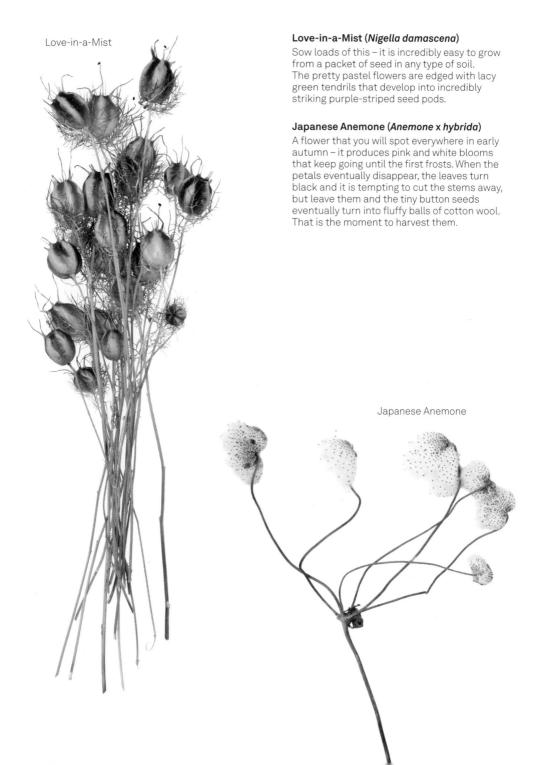

Love-in-a-Mist

Love-in-a-Mist (*Nigella damascena*)

Sow loads of this – it is incredibly easy to grow from a packet of seed in any type of soil. The pretty pastel flowers are edged with lacy green tendrils that develop into incredibly striking purple-striped seed pods.

Japanese Anemone (*Anemone* x *hybrida*)

A flower that you will spot everywhere in early autumn – it produces pink and white blooms that keep going until the first frosts. When the petals eventually disappear, the leaves turn black and it is tempting to cut the stems away, but leave them and the tiny button seeds eventually turn into fluffy balls of cotton wool. That is the moment to harvest them.

Japanese Anemone

Lenten Roses

Michaelmas Daisy

Michaelmas Daisy (*Symphyotrichum*)

The tiny star-like flowers of asters herald the start of autumn. You can find them in the wild or grow them in your garden. The flowers fade as the first frosts appear, but leave them and by mid-winter you can harvest the beautiful seed heads.

Lenten Roses (*Helleborus*)

One of the earliest perennial flowers of the gardening year, heralding the end of winter. Pick them as the inner petals die back and you can see a seed head appearing. Remove any outer petals as they fade and turn blotchy.

Pasque Flower (*Pulsatilla vulgaris*)

You may spot these growing in the wild in sheltered areas. They are also easy to grow as small plants in the garden. The delicate purple flowers develop gorgeous silvery heads after putting on a show of colour in the spring.

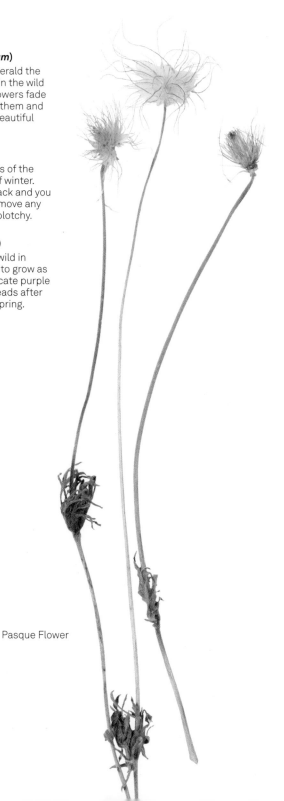

Pasque Flower

Lamb's Ear (*Stachys byzantina*)

Commonly grown as a ground cover because of its beautiful rosette-forming mounds of velvety silver leaves. Its tall purple flowers appear as spearheads, and when the petals die back their form remains wonderfully intact.

Vervain (*Verbena*)

An easy-to-grow upright perennial plant, good for container growing. It bears tight clusters of flowers in bright jewel-like colours. In autumn these give way to delicate seed heads that remain intact.

Teasel (*Dipsacus*)

A biennial to grow from seed – you just have to be patient and wait for the attractive but prickly spiked heads to appear. It is invaluable for dried arrangements, because it seems to last forever. You can also forage for teasels in the wild, but remember to wear gloves: the spiny stems are impossible to handle otherwise.

Teasel

Lamb's Ear

Vervain

Black-Eyed Susan (*Rudbeckia hirta*) and Coneflower (*Echinacea*)

These easy-to-grow perennials aren't fussy about their situation. Grow in pots or small spaces for their daisy-like flowers, which come in a rainbow of colours. Every variety has an attractive dark, spiky centre, where the seeds form. As the petals dry off, this is the part you want to harvest and keep.

Bear's Breeches (*Acanthus mollis*)

The tall, spiky white flowers of this hardy perennial turn into elegant seed heads with a purple tinge. Display as single stems.

Grape Hyacinth (*Muscari*)

You can't miss the tiny, bright blue, cone-shaped flowers of grape hyacinths growing everywhere in springtime. Grow them from bulbs planted the previous autumn – they are perfect for pots. As the blue fades, the seed heads keep their shape. Harvest them in early summer.

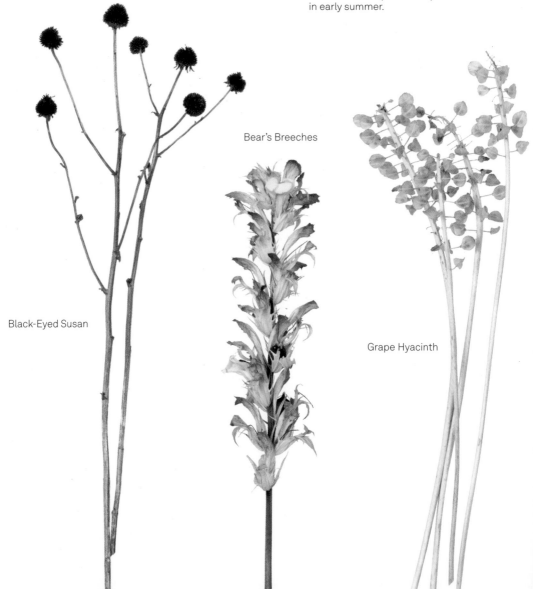

Bear's Breeches

Black-Eyed Susan

Grape Hyacinth

Opium Poppy (*Papaver somniferum*)
All varieties of poppy produce wonderful seed pods. Although their flowers are fleeting and often last only a day, their pods last for years. Growing a few different varieties will provide you with pods of different sizes to create a stunning monotype arrangement.

Montbretia (*Crocosmia*)

A hardy perennial that spreads quickly in the garden and can also be found growing wild. Its erect, funnel-shaped flowers appear in late summer and early autumn in hues of red and orange, dying back to form seeds in tiny brown balls intricately strung together.

Honesty (*Lunaria annua*)

This is strictly a biennial, not an annual as the name suggests. It is worth growing for the almost translucent pockets that eventually appear from its unassuming purple flowers. Sow it at the back of a mixed border and forget about it – you will have a delightful surprise two seasons later.

Honesty

Montbretia

Jacaranda (*Jacaranda*)

Jacaranda trees flourish in the southern hemisphere, where they drip with the most amazing lavender-coloured flowers in the spring. Walking underneath them is a thrill, and with luck you'll find some fallen seed pods lying on the ground.

HIPS AND BERRIES

Many flowering plants and shrubs produce hips and berries as part of their life cycle. These small colourful fruits contain seeds that guarantee their continued survival. Harvesting them from wild hedgerows and our gardens in the autumn and early winter provides us with a direct connection to nature. They can be dried and preserved temporarily to create seasonal festive arrangements.

Hips should be harvested for preserving and drying in late summer and early autumn. Look for those that are plump and firm to the touch just as the leaves are dropping. Wearing gloves to handle thorny stems, cut bunches of hips off with a sharp knife and remove any remaining foliage from the lower stems. Preserve them in a glycerine solution, which will prevent the hips from turning mushy or mouldy. Then air-dry; they will wrinkle but retain their lovely colour.

- Garden-grown rambling roses produce some of the best hips **(2, 4)**: look out especially for *Rosa filipes* 'Kiftsgate', *R.* 'Rambling Rector', *R.* 'The Garland' and *R.* 'Bobbie James'.
- Forage for dog rose (*Rosa canina*) or wild rose (*R. rugosa*) hips growing freely in country hedgerows.
- Dried hips can be combined with other dried flowers, added to winter wreaths or tied to seasonal gifts for decoration.

Ornamental berries are small, brightly coloured, pulpy fruits that grow on a plant from single flowers. These berries should not be confused with edible fruits; some are poisonous if consumed. Always wear gloves to handle them and wash your hands afterwards.

For drying, choose berries that appear in clusters formed from florets. Preserve berries in a glycerine solution, or experiment with air-drying, heat-drying or sand-drying. The fleshier the berry, the longer it will take to dry out. Ultimately, berries will wrinkle, but they will retain their colour.

- Ornamental berries make attractive dried material: try adding berries of eucalyptus (*Eucalyptus*), both young **(1, 5)** and mature **(3)**; St John's wort (*Hypericum*); heavenly bamboo (*Nandina domestica*); or ivy (*Hedera*) to your displays.

FRUIT AND VEGETABLES

Many types of everyday fruit and vegetables make interesting dried materials. As long as decomposition has not started, experiment with drying your leftover fruit and vegetables instead of throwing them away.

Fruit

Fruit can be arranged with nuts, candles and dried or fresh flowers to create still-life displays for special occasions. Choose whole fruits with a firm outer skin: citrus fruits, passion fruit and pomegranates give the best results. Leave them in an airing cupboard or equivalent for a couple of weeks to ensure that all the moisture disappears, or dry them in the oven (see pages 114–15). You will find that during the drying process the skins harden and change colour.

Here are some ways in which you can experiment with different kinds of fruit:

- Gild or spray-paint oranges and pomegranates once they are completely dry.
- Make festive decorations by slicing grapefruits, oranges, lemons and limes and drying the slices individually on a tray overnight in a warm room or in the oven on a very low heat. Make a hole in the rind with a skewer while it is still fresh, and thread through with a length of ribbon or string.
- Do the same with apple slices to reveal the pattern created by the core. Dab with lemon juice to prevent them from going brown.
- Bunches of crab apples harvested in autumn will keep their colour and remain firm for many weeks after drinking a solution of glycerine.
- Buy or forage for wild quinces in autumn and leave to dry in a warm room: their perfume is delicious.

Vegetables

Vegetables can also be dried and incorporated into interesting displays. Vegetables such as gourds, chillies and artichokes can be dried whole, or you can experiment with different parts of the plants: flowers, foliage, stalks and husks.

- The leaves of any leafy green vegetable from the cabbage *(Brassica)* family dry to perfection. They shrink as they dry, but retain their colour. Use the outer leaves that you would normally discard when cooking, lay them on a tray and dry in the oven on a very low heat overnight.

- If you grow your own broccoli or kale and find that it has bolted, air-dry the flower stalks.

- Forage for the flower heads and leaves of rapeseed *(Brassica napus)*. You'll see it growing all over the place in early summer. Long stems bearing its tiny yellow flowers can be air-dried.

- Miniature purple artichokes dry out naturally over time – try growing them and harvest before they are fully mature.

- Ornamental gourds, related to the pumpkin family, are easy to grow from seed for harvesting in the autumn. In the run-up to Halloween you will find them on market stalls or in the supermarket.

- Grow chillies indoors from seed for culinary use: they will turn from green to red as they ripen, and they look beautiful hanging in bunches to dry.

- Find ornamental sweetcorn in farmers' markets, or buy heirloom seeds and grow it yourself in pots; the mixed colours are gorgeous and the husks dry out naturally.

- Beans, peas and other legumes all dry out to add extra interest. Choose those with interesting colours and patterns.

- Loofahs make fantastic dried material. You can grow them from seed in the same fashion as cucumbers, and as young plants they are edible. Left to mature and wrinkle, the outer skin can be removed to reveal the dry, coarse, fibrous matter inside.

EXOTICS

I love the idea of 'holiday flowers', dried or pressed as a memento of other cultures and climates. When I travel, I get a thrill from looking at the indigenous flora of other countries, and I visit flower shops and markets to see what I can dry to bring home. It's nice to have a display that evokes another time and place.

What seems exotic to me are the richly coloured flowers of tropical and more temperate regions, since I know they won't stand a chance in my own garden in the northern hemisphere. Depending on where you live, there will be other flowers that tick this box, but the principle is the same.

While it is illegal to import live plants, there is nothing to stop you from wrapping a few dried stems in newspaper or tissue and packing them in your suitcase. Being effectively dead, they are no longer a risk in terms of carrying pests or disease.

Because the cut-flower industry is global, you can also source imported flowers for drying at home, and if you are planning to use them for a long-lasting display, the carbon footprint is slightly less troubling.

Naturally harvested sea sponges and seaweed also make interesting additions to any dried display and look wonderfully exotic. Sea sponges are easily sourced in Greece, where they are harvested sustainably, or you can buy them online; they are ready-dried, so just don't get them wet.

Seaweeds and underwater flowers represent a whole new world of fascinating plants that are yet to be really discovered. Some pretty dried pieces styled with a few shells and pebbles make a holiday keepsake long after your tan has disappeared.

Fynbos Flowers

The Fynbos is a small ecoregion on the Western Cape of South Africa. The plants that grow there are primarily small flowering shrubs and evergreens. The flowers, collectively known as 'Fynbos flowers', are harvested for export and can be purchased for drying. Air-dry.

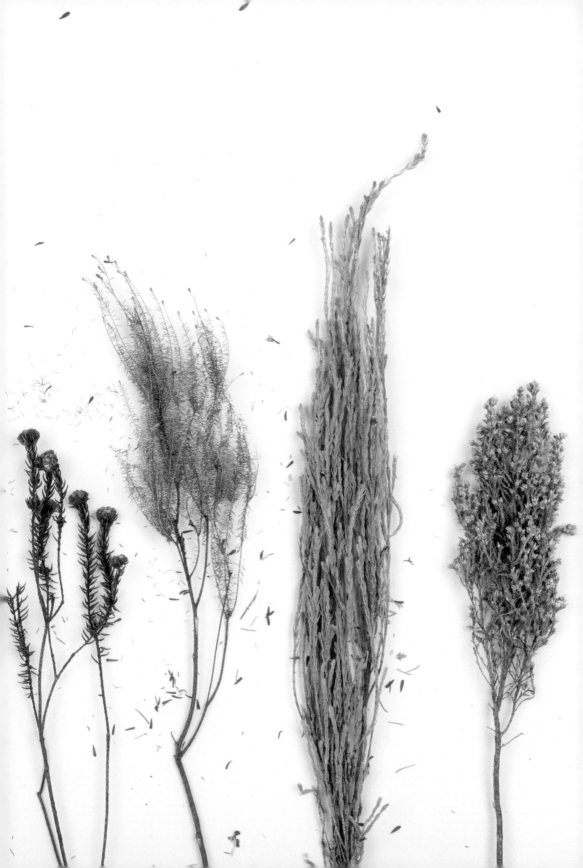

Crane Flower or Bird of Paradise (*Strelitzia reginae*)

These brightly coloured blooms from South Africa (so called because they resemble a bird's beak) will fade gradually over time as they dry, but their intriguing form and shape will remain intact. Vase-dry.

Flower of Maryam (*Anastatica hierochuntica*)

You'll find this strangely beautiful dried flower in the souks of North Africa and the Middle East, where it is ground into a paste and used for medicine. It is harvested from the desert, where it adapts to arid conditions by curling up into a tight ball until it the rain comes, when it flowers temporarily before drying again.

Lotus (*Nelumbo nucifera*)

It is easy to see why the breathtaking flowers of the lotus plant are revered throughout Asia and India. While the flowers are not suitable for drying, the seed pods are a feat of natural engineering with their flat-topped heads divided into tiny individual compartments. You can find them freshly cut and green in flower shops and dry them at home, where they will turn dark brown. Vase-dry.

Palms (Arecaceae family)

The palm family is a group of shrubs and trees that are predominantly native to tropical and sub-tropical climates, but it is possible to grow certain varieties in colder temperature zones. Their leaves make fantastic dried material when trimmed to shape; palm fruits and panicles also dry very well.

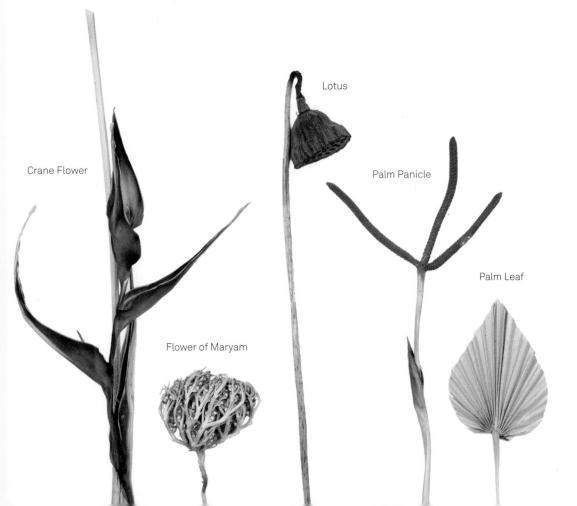

Crane Flower

Lotus

Palm Panicle

Palm Leaf

Flower of Maryam

Grow Your Own

The most effective way to build up a collection
of dried flowers is to grow your own. If you're
experienced at growing garden flowers to pick for
fresh arrangements, it's not much of a leap. If you're
a complete novice and new to gardening, it's a fun,
easy and inexpensive way to get stuck in. You'll
experience enormous pride and satisfaction when
you harvest your blooms to dry.

Sowing Seeds: What, When and How

Growing your own plants has wide ecological and environmental benefits: filling an outside space with flowers means you'll be offering a home to bees and other pollinators that in turn will attract birds and other wildlife. You'll enjoy a connection with nature that only comes from tending and nurturing tiny plants.

Annuals put all their energy into flowering in one season and are particularly easy to grow from seed. They don't develop deep root systems, and so are ideal for growing in small spaces and pots. They are also good for larger spaces, especially if you want to start a flower patch from scratch without spending a fortune. Once they have finished flowering, they will die back, never to flower again from the same parent plant; they will, however, set seed that you can collect to sow again the following year.

Annuals are either hardy or half-hardy. This determines when and where to sow your seed; instructions on individual seed packets will give you this information. Hardy annuals can withstand freezing temperatures, so you can sow them directly into the ground in autumn or spring. Sowing in the autumn will mean they'll flower earlier in the summer of the following year. Seeds sown in the spring will flower the same summer, but slightly later in the season. By splitting a packet of hardy annual seeds and sowing half in autumn and half the next spring, you'll get a succession of flowers that takes you through the whole summer. Half-hardy annuals are tender plants and won't withstand freezing conditions; you can sow them indoors and plant them outside when any chance of a frost has passed, or wait and sow outdoors when the weather has warmed up.

Biennials are plants that behave like annuals but do not flower until the second season after sowing, so they require a bit more time and patience.

Perennials live for several years and will come back reliably from the same parent. They can be hardy or tender. Hardy types can withstand freezing temperatures; the top growth will die back in winter, but the roots survive underground. Tender perennials may need some protection from cold.

Both the roots and the top growth of perennial plants spread over time. By lifting and dividing them at the roots as they get bigger, you can create new plants for free. Grow perennials from seed in the same way as annuals, or buy them as seedlings or plug plants from nurseries at the beginning of the growing season and plant them directly into the ground or a pot, which will guarantee quicker flowering. As soon as the soil and air warm up, they will put on growth really quickly, providing you with plenty of material to harvest for drying right through to the autumn. Many perennial flowers turn into wonderful seed heads for drying, so resist the temptation to deadhead.

Opposite Perfect plants to grow yourself: poppy and ornamental onion (centre) for seed heads, with herbs lemon balm (foreground) and fennel (background), along with quaking grass (left).

GROW YOUR OWN FLOWERS

The following instructions use annual drumstick scabious (*Scabiosa stellata* 'Sternkugel') as an example, but they will work for most kinds of seeds. Both the pincushion-shaped flowers and the papery seed pods of scabious make perfect drying material.

1. Sowing

Fill a recycled or reusable plastic seed tray almost to the top with seed compost. Using your fingers, poke the seeds gently into the compost, spacing them evenly, and cover over. Water gently, just enough to moisten. Set the seed tray aside in a light place; a window ledge is ideal. Seeds need warmth and light to germinate. Be sure to keep the compost damp, misting or watering gently as it dries out.

2. Seedlings

After 10–14 days you will see signs of germination. Tiny seedlings with a pair of dark green leaves will gradually make their way through the compost to reach the light. As they put on a little height, they need a chance to acclimatize or 'harden off'. On a warm day put the tray outside, but bring it in again at night.

3. Pricking out

Wait until each seedling has developed at least one more set of leaves and put on some height, ideally to about 5 centimetres (2.5 inches) tall. They are now ready to 'prick out', which means transplanting each individual seedling into its own pot, so that both the roots and leaves have space to grow without encumbrance. Look for biodegradable coir pots rather than plastic.

Fill pots with potting compost and make a hole in the compost with your finger or a blunt pencil to just below halfway. Use a blunt-edged knife or a teaspoon to scoop each seedling from the bottom of the seed tray without damaging the tiny roots. Hold it by its leaves and place it securely in its new home, firming compost around the roots, and water.

4. Planting

Move your seedlings to a safe place outside and keep watering regularly. When they have put on enough bushy growth to fill the coir pots, plant them directly into the ground or put several plants into a much larger pot or tub filled with compost. Dig a hole slightly bigger than the pot, then place the pot in the hole and firm the compost around the base of the plant. The roots will grow through the coir pots, which will decompose naturally into the compost after a couple of months.

5. Cutting and drying

As your plants put on yet more growth, you will see the delicate, pale flower heads appearing. Harvest some of them individually for drying at this stage. Regular cutting will encourage new flowers. Leave the remaining flowers on the stems and watch them turn into beautiful seed pods that are a work of art. Cut these when they feel firm to the touch and arrange them with the dried flower heads.

GROW YOUR OWN GRASSES

Quaking grass (*Briza media*) is the easiest grass in the world to grow. It's strictly an annual, but because of its self-seeding habit you'll find it comes back year after year and you'll never be without it.

1. Sowing

Sow seed thinly in a tray, as for flowers; the seed is tiny, so it must be sprinkled between your fingers or scattered directly on to the ground where you want it to grow. Stagger the sowing times so that you have new plants germinating throughout the growing season, and keep back any unused seed for next year.

2. Planting

Germination is very quick, and you'll soon see what look like blades of thin grass poking through the compost. As soon as they are big enough to handle, transfer your seedlings to a larger pot or plant them straight into a bed; the grass makes a great filler for any gaps between flowers.

3. Cutting and drying

As your plants put on growth, you will notice the tiny heads appearing; they look like raindrops as they catch the light. Allow for maximum growth and cut with abundance. Replace harvested material with new seedlings during the growing season and make your final cut before the first frosts.

GROW YOUR OWN
SEED PODS

Honesty (*Lunaria annua*)
is commonly known as the
money plant or moon plant
because of its fabulous seed
pods. Its seeds are about the
size of a baby's fingernail
and can be sown directly
into individual pots or
straight into the ground.

1. Sowing

Sow in early autumn and/or spring for a good succession of strong, healthy plants. Plants sown in the autumn will germinate quickly in warm soil and put on rapid growth as soon as the weather warms up again. Honesty is a biennial, so plants will not flower until the following year. You need to be patient.

2. Seed pods

After a year, in late spring/early summer, clusters of purple flowers will appear and gradually fade. As the petals fall away, you'll see the beginnings of the young seed pods, green-mauve in colour, with tiny seeds inside. Allow them to mature on the plant, stripping away any foliage as it turns brown.

3. Cutting and drying

When you can see that the pods have stopped getting bigger, and they are starting to feel dry and the seeds inside are brown, cut the stems from the plant. You'll notice that the pods are starting to crack and peel, and you need to continue this process very gently, removing the outer layer of green from the pod to reveal the translucent skin underneath. In doing this you'll also dislodge the seeds. Store them in an envelope in a dry place and you can start the cycle over again by repeat-planting in the autumn to ensure a continuous supply of plant material. At this stage, take a moment to marvel mindfully at the wonder of nature and its bounty.

Honesty's Latin name, *Lunaria*, means 'moon-shaped', referring to the plant's round seed pods. When dried, they make striking arrangements.

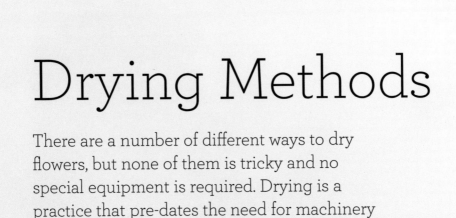

Drying Methods

There are a number of different ways to dry flowers, but none of them is tricky and no special equipment is required. Drying is a practice that pre-dates the need for machinery or technology. In this day and age, it is lovely to be able to turn our hands to something so simple and uncomplicated with such beautifully productive rewards.

Tried and Tested Techniques

The key to successful drying is to use flower and plant material that is as fresh as possible, with minimal time lost between harvesting and the start of the drying process.

If you want to dry shop-bought flowers, avoid any that are not in their normal growing season. The commercial cut-flower industry is a huge global enterprise, in which flowers grown for year-round availability are transported as commodities from one side of the world to the other. Any flowers that have been picked and packed in cold storage for a long journey can be tricky to dry satisfactorily. Their heads will wilt as soon as they are out of water, and their fragile necks have a tendency to snap.

If it's not possible to grow everything yourself, follow the seasons of the country in which you live and purchase locally grown flowers for drying. The upside of this is that your dried flowers will have a low carbon footprint and you'll feel more connected with the natural environment. Ask your florist for guidance and determine the provenance of any flowers before buying. A visit to an independent flower farm gives you the chance to pick exactly what you want, or you can place orders online for next-day delivery.

AIR DRYING

Recommended for all types of cut flowers and foliage with stems intact, air drying is the most straightforward way to dry freshly picked flowers. It is a totally natural method that encourages all the moisture within the component parts of a flower (stem, leaves, head and petals) to evaporate over time. Note that thick bushy stems will take several weeks to dry out completely, whereas a single wispy stem will dry in a matter of days.

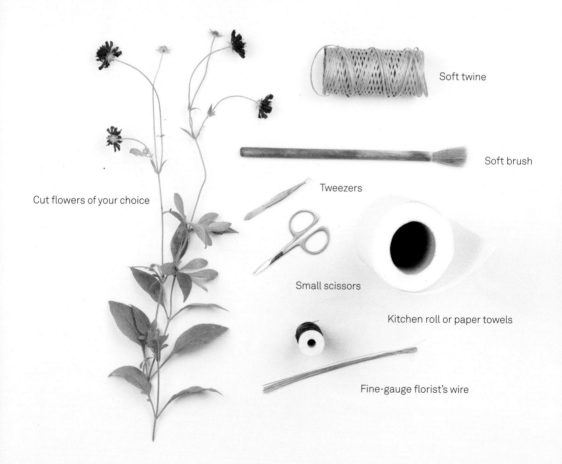

Soft twine

Soft brush

Tweezers

Cut flowers of your choice

Small scissors

Kitchen roll or paper towels

Fine-gauge florist's wire

1. Select your flowers
Remember that the drying process reduces the volume of flowers by 50 to 70 per cent, so if you are looking to create arrangements for specific vases or hand-tied bunches, you will need a lot more dried flowers to work with than you would fresh ones.

2. Remove excess moisture
Once you have picked or bought your flowers, lay them out on a flat surface and remove as much moisture as possible by dabbing them with absorbent paper or kitchen roll. Give each stem a full inspection and remove any damaged petals, traces of soil or tiny insects with a pair of tweezers.

3. Prepare your plant
Using a small pair of sharp scissors, trim off the lower leaves so you have at least 12 centimetres (5 inches) of bare stem; if the ends of the stems are very soft and mushy, reduce them.

4. Attach your twine
Take a length of soft twine, fine-gauge florist's wire or a rubber band, and secure it gently around the bare stem, leaving enough flexibility so you can easily attach the stem to a hook or peg. If your stems are very thin and wispy, you can put several together to create a slim bunch at slightly different heights; just make sure the heads are not touching.

5. Hang your flowers to dry

Suspend your flowers head down in a dry space where they can stay undisturbed for as long as the process takes. Avoid placing them in direct sunlight, because the colours will bleach out. I use S-hooks to hang them from the sides of my kitchen cabinets, or you can tie them on to wire coat hangers or a length of twine. Any available pegs or hooks around the house, or a wooden laundry dryer or clothes rail, are all incredibly useful for drying flowers. The main thing is to create enough room for the air to circulate around the whole stem and to keep them bone dry. If they get damp, or there is insufficient air, they will go mouldy and rot. If you see this happening in one bunch, or even one flower, discard it immediately, or the mould will spread quickly to other bunches.

6. Remove when ready

The heads will droop at first, but don't panic: the drying process starts at the base of the stem, which will soon become brittle to the touch. You will know the whole flower is ready to take down when it starts to feel brittle and crispy. Remove them from their hooks very gently, as the necks are delicate and will snap quite easily. With deft handling you will have flowers to style and arrange for your home that will last and last.

DRYING ON THE STEM

Recommended for seed heads and grasses, this method is really just a case of waiting for any plant material to dry out naturally on its stem before you pick it.

1. Watch for seed heads in the garden
In the garden, leave the dying heads on flowers to allow seed heads to form. Keep an eye on them as they gradually turn from green to brown. Feel them and notice as they start to become slightly brittle to the touch; they are ready to harvest when the heads and stems are still firm but contain no moisture.

Forage for seed heads
If you are foraging, do it in the autumn, when the seed heads of most wild flowers are ripe and grasses are ready for harvesting. Take sharp secateurs, and gloves for prickly heads such as teasels (*Dipsacus*), and pick stems here and there without denuding a whole plant. Take a shallow basket or trug with you so that you can lay harvested material flat.

2. Harvest stems
Make a clean cut at the base of the stem with a pair of sharp secateurs, and remove any brown or dead foliage. Lay your harvested stems out flat, or stand them upright in a dry bucket, keeping the heads separated. Handle everything very carefully: drying seed heads are extremely fragile and will snap easily.

3. Display or store your seed heads
Keep the seed heads attached to their stems. Use them for immediate display and let them continue to dry over time, or wrap them in tissue paper and store carefully until required.

VASE DRYING

Although it might seem counterintuitive to dry flowers in water, some varieties actually dry more effectively if they are placed in a small amount of water. Freshly picked flowers with heads clustered with florets (tiny individual flowers), such as hydrangeas (*Hydrangea*), baby's breath (*Gypsophila*), ornamental onions (*Allium*), bishop's weed (*Ammi majus*) and astrantia (*Astrantia*), all respond well to this treatment.

1. Prepare your flowers
Lay out the flowers and inspect them. Discard any foliage, and cut 1 centimetre (half an inch) off the stems.

2. Select a vase
Use a vase tall enough to support the stems up to the flower necks. Pour clean, cold water into the vase to a depth of about 5 centimetres (2 inches).

3. Monitor the water
Refresh the water as necessary and keep it clean, as any bacteria will kill the flowers; add a drop of bleach to prevent this. Over a week or so, the stems will start to yellow and you will notice the flower heads begin to dry. Once the flower heads are dry to the touch, remove them from the water and trim away the wet stem ends. Display or store.

SAND DRYING

Sand drying is recommended for heavy flower heads. It is the oldest known drying technique, used by the ancient Egyptians, and the only method that preserves perfume. Try it for lemon-scented pelargoniums (such as *Pelargonium* 'Bitter Lemon') and sweetly fragranced pinks (*Dianthus*), or flowers that have big, fleshy heads, such as ranunculus (*Ranunculus*), carnations (*Dianthus caryophyllus*) and peonies (*Paeonia*) when fully open.

1. Prepare a container

Find a sturdy box, a deep bowl such as a washing-up bowl, or another suitable container. Fill it a quarter of the way full with a level layer of clean, dry, fine washed sand (children's play sand is ideal). Note that sand is heavy: it is better to use several small containers than one very large one if you want to move them after filling.

2. Prepare your flowers

Inspect the flowers for browning petals, insect damage and so on, and remove any that are less than perfect. Then cut away the stem so that you are left with a head and no other parts. Place the heads, evenly spaced, on top of the sand, gently wedging them in. Use a jug or cup to pour more sand over and around the flower heads until they are completely covered, making sure they stay in shape with sand between the open petals.

3. Monitor the petals

Set aside in a warm, dry place for a minimum of two weeks; the process can take longer, but keep checking and leave until the petals are crisp. Remove the flowers from the sand, shaking them gently, and brush away any remaining particles with a soft paintbrush. The sand can be reused as required.

Using silica instead of sand

Silica is a non-toxic, odourless chemical that works as a desiccant (you find sachets of it inside newly purchased items such as shoes or leather bags to prevent them from getting damp), and it can be used as an alternative to sand drying. Silica is manufactured as tiny white beads that you can buy in large bags online. It is harmless, but avoid using it around small children, as the beads are a choking hazard.

Follow the same process as for sand drying. Silica is lighter than sand, so you can fill larger containers, but make sure they are airtight and use a lid. It also works more quickly than sand, and some flowers will take only a couple of days to dry.

DRYING BY DIRECT HEAT SOURCE

Commercially produced dried flowers are dehydrated by machine. You can more or less replicate this method at home by drying via a direct heat source, such as a microwave or conventional oven, which is particularly suitable for fruit. You can combine air drying and heat-source drying with an airing cupboard or hot press, a boiler room or sufficient space directly above a radiator or heater.

Drying rack

1. Prepare and suspend your flowers

If you want to dry flowers on an ongoing basis, it's worth installing some kind of permanent drying rack. You can buy one specifically for the purpose or construct something yourself. Follow the instructions for air drying to prepare and string up your flowers (see pages 104–6). Suspend them upside down.

2. Monitor your flowers

Your flowers will dry more quickly in the heat than through regular air drying, so keep checking them; if you leave them too long they'll become desiccated and you won't be able to handle them without them crumbling.

Conventional oven

1. Prepare your fruit

Fruit dries best in a conventional (gas/electric/fan) oven. Slice citrus fruit such as tangerines, oranges, lemons and limes to about 1 centimetre (half an inch) thick. Be sure to pierce a small hole in the rind with a skewer if you want to suspend the slices once they are dry. Then space the slices out on a tray covered in greaseproof paper. You can also place whole fruit in the oven to dry.

2. Heat your fruit

Set the oven to the lowest temperature and leave the fruit until all the juices and moisture have evaporated. Remove and leave to cool – the fruit will harden off. If you plan to suspend your dried fruit slices, thread twine or ribbon through the hole you made in the rind before they are completely hard. Whole fruit will take longer to dry than sliced fruit, so leave it overnight if necessary.

Microwave oven

1. Prepare your flowers
You can dry flower heads and detached petals in a microwave oven. This is effective if you want to dry a lot of tiny flowers or petals quickly. Remove the stems and place the heads or petals directly on to the glass plate.

2. Heat your flowers
Start heating the flowers in five-second bursts on the lowest setting. Repeat until they are crisp to the touch but still retain their colour. If they turn brown, you have overdone it. When you are finished, make a note of the total time for repeating the exercise.

PRESSING

Pressing flowers is an activity that can be taken to many different levels. You can buy professional flower presses for the purpose, or make your own using sheets of thin card layered between two pieces of plywood and bound together with thick ribbon. The easiest and simplest way to press flowers is between the pages of books.

1. Select and inspect your plants
Before pressing, dry and inspect the flowers or leaves, removing any damaged or brown parts.

2. Position your plants
Place double sheets of newspaper or blotting paper between two pages of a thick book, and position your flowers, some face up and some face down. Use tweezers to unfurl any petals or leaves that refuse to lie flat. Check you are happy with the presentation and positioning.

3. Press your plants
Close the book, securing it with two wide rubber bands. Do not open for at least two weeks: tempting as it is to check your specimens, they will move if they are not completely dry. After two weeks or more, your flowers will take on a papery quality. When they are ready, mount them under glass, use them for making cards and gift tags, or tape them gently onto a plain white wall to create a mural (see page 162). Use large petals, such as rose petals, to make a flower shape when mounting.

à Mlle Choin. Il le lui dit, et lui montra une lettre
cachetée pour elle qui en faisoit mention, pour lui
être rendue s'il mésarrivoit de lui. Elle fut extrême-
ment sensible, comme il est aisé de le juger, à une
marque d'affection de cette prévoyance, mais elle
n'eut point de repos qu'elle ne lui eût fait mettre
devant elle le testament et la lettre au feu ; et pro-
testa que si elle avoit le malheur de lui survivre, mille
écus de rente qu'elle avoit amassés seroient encore
trop pour elle. Après cela il est surprenant qu'il ne se
soit trouvé aucune disposition dans les papiers de
Monseigneur.

Quelque dure qu'ait été son éducation, il avoit
conservé de l'amitié et de la considération pour le
célèbre évêque de Meaux, et un vrai respect pour
la mémoire du duc de Montausier, tant il est vrai
que la vertu se fait honorer des hommes malgré leur
goût et leur amour de l'indépendance et de la liberté.
Monseigneur n'étoit pas même insensible au plaisir
de la marquer à tout ce qui étoit de sa famille, et
jusqu'aux anciens domestiques qu'il lui avoit connus.
C'est peut-être une des choses qui a le plus soutenu
d'Antin auprès de lui dans les diverses aventures de
sa vie, dont la femme étoit fille de la duchesse d'Uzès,
fille unique du duc de Montausier, et qu'il aimoit
passionnément. Il le marqua encore à Sainte-Maure,
qui, embarrassé dans ses affaires sur le point de se
marier, reçut une pension de Monseigneur sans
l'avoir demandée, avec ces obligeantes paroles, mais
qui faisoient tant d'honneur au prince : « qu'il ne
manqueroit jamais au nom et au neveu de M. de
Montausier. » Sainte-Maure se montra digne de cette
grâce. Son mariage se rompit, et il ne s'est jamais
marié. Il remit la pension qui n'étoit donnée qu'en
faveur du mariage. Monseigneur la reprit ; je ne dirai
pas qu'il eût mieux fait de la lui laisser.

C'étoit peut-être le seul homme de qualité qu'il
aida de sa poche. Aussi tenoit-il à lui par des
dences, tandis qu'il eut des maîtresses, qu
lui souffrit guère. En leur place, il eut
soulagements passagers et obscurs de
teries, dont il étoit peu capable, et c
Francine, gendre de Lulli, et qu
ensemble l'Opéra, lui fournirent

La Raisin, fameuse comédienne
seule de celles-là qui dura
On la ménageoit, et le m
âge et avec sa dé
l'aller voir, et de lu
table tout ce qu'il y
fants de toutes ces sortes
fille de celle-ci, même
Chaillot, chez le
depuis sa mort par
en prit soin
après. Cette
mit fin à tous
de la bâtardise, il
reconnu
jamais pu
nagé dans les
en peine et
toute sa vie
plaice à lui
règulièrement
d'Antin et le
d'atours, mais
en petit les deux
rand M. le prince de
Conti et M.   ducs de Luxembourg,
Villeroy et de   en, et ceux-là sur un

Pressed flower artwork by MR Studio London

Wide, flat-headed flower varieties such as pansies, primroses, ox-eye daisies and sunflowers press well, along with annuals that flatten easily, such as cornflowers, marigolds and poppies. You can also press grasses and wispy wild flowers on the stem, ferns, or richly coloured autumn leaves, whose veined detail is exposed during the process.

PRESERVING WITH GLYCERINE

Glycerine is available from chemists and pharmacies as a skincare product. It is synthetically produced as a moisturizer, drawing moisture from the air to keep the outer layer of skin firm and plump. It does the same with berries and hips, slowing down the wrinkling process so they will continue to look good in dried displays long after they have been picked. It is recommended for drying rose (*Rosa*) hips; berries such as St John's wort (*Hypericum*), viburnum (*Viburnum*), elderberry (*Sambucus*) and berried ivy (*Hedera*); and autumnal foliage such as copper beech (*Fagus sylvatica* f. *purpurea*) leaves.

1. Dissolve the glycerine

Mix one part glycerine with two parts warm water in a vase or jug to the halfway point, and stir well until the glycerine is fully dissolved.

2. Prepare the berries

Remove the foliage from rose hip and berry stems. Recut the stems to expose fresh new cells that will drink freely.

3. Arrange the stems

Arrange the stems in the glycerine solution so they are not touching or overlapping, and leave them immersed for a week or so. Remove and combine with dried flowers for seasonal arrangements.

Handling and Storing Dried Flowers

Now that you're growing and drying your own plants, you'll quickly get used to handling dried flowers. If you've been successful in growing and drying a lot of flowers, make sure to hold some back to add to your displays later or to give away in place of a fresh bouquet.

If you're more familiar with arranging fresh flowers, you'll notice a big difference when you begin working with dried material. Here are a few tips to help you avoid some common pitfalls:

- Dried flowers have no flexibility – their stems are rigid – and if you try to twist or bend them they will snap. Garden-picked flowers will keep their natural curves and bends when you hang them up to dry, so be sure to include these in your displays if you don't like the ramrod-straight look.

- It's not easy to wire dried flowers, so unless you are an experienced florist, don't try too hard to create complicated or difficult arrangements. You're more likely to break the heads if you over-handle them.

- If you have dried a largish bunch of thin, wispy stems together, use them like this in your display. Don't try to separate the stems; they will have dried as a mass and will only break if you attempt to take them apart.

- Attend a dried flower workshop if you want to get some practice before you start handling your own – lots of professional florists offer these.

If you have more dried flowers than you need for your current project, keep your leftovers in storage so that you can reach for them easily when inspiration strikes again:

- Wrap unused stems singly or in small untied bunches in unbleached tissue or plain brown paper.

- Lay wrapped flowers flat in a large drawer or shallow cardboard box. Stack gently with heads and stems in alternating directions. They'll keep for ages and ages.

- Store in a dry, cool place, away from direct sunlight.

Styling

The key to styling dried flowers in a modern way is to keep it simple. Consider texture, shape and colour: choose textures and shapes that contrast and colours in similar hues, or mix up your colours and stick with flowers of similar shapes and textures. Don't combine too many different elements – less is definitely more when it comes to contemporary arrangements.

Decorative Techniques

Dried materials are beautiful in their own right, but you can decorate them further for a variety of colourful effects. Painting, spraying and dyeing are three decorative techniques that you can apply to dried plants before adding them to displays.

Experiment to see how colouring your dried materials can add to your arrangements:

- Bright green paint can bring brown, decayed palm leaves (Arecaceae family) or similar large leaves back to life.

- Chalky matt paints in different tones of natural hues can turn a dead branch into a thing of beauty.

- Try spraying large and small dry flower heads, seed heads, grasses and bunches of foliage, choosing a range of complementary colours to create a bespoke display that works with your interior decor.

- Spray tiny leaves and flowers in pearlescent or metallic paint to prevent them from getting lost in a large arrangement – they'll stand out so you can appreciate them more.

- Dyeing large quantities of dried material can be fiddly and time-consuming, but they are also available to buy commercially in a rainbow of colours.

- If you want to experiment with making your own natural dyes, there are lots of suggestions online and you'll know that no chemicals have been used in the process. Beetroot, tea, turmeric and saffron all work as natural dye solutions, or you can use shop-bought natural food dyes.

DYEING

Although dyeing, a wet process, may seem counterintuitive when working with dried material, the following method works if the material is sturdy enough to resist being submerged in water. Teasels (*Dipsacus*) and similar seed heads, grasses such as wheat (*Triticum*) and barley (*Hordeum vulgare*), and dry mosses and sponges are all good candidates for this treatment.

1. Add dye to water

To a vase of cold water, add a natural dye solution in your chosen colour, or some food colouring. The more colour you add, the more intense the result will be. Stir well.

2. Submerge your dried plants

Plunge the material into the water, upside down if you are dyeing seed heads or grasses. Leave in the solution until you see that the colour has taken; a few hours is usually enough.

3. Remove and dry

Remove the material and blot dry on kitchen towel or absorbent paper. When all the excess moisture has been removed, hang in a bunch upside down or stand in a clean dry vase to allow everything to dry completely. If you are dyeing mosses or sponges, gently squeeze out the excess water and leave to dry naturally. Your colour solution can be reused straight away or bottled and kept in the fridge for later.

PAINTING

Large leaves – particularly palm (Arecaceae family) – and stems of foliage can be painted for both naturalistic and artificial effect. Try using up unfinished cans of wall paint or buy tester pots to experiment with different colours.

1. Prepare your material

Wait until the leaves have lost their chlorophyll and turned completely brown through the drying process, as they will be more absorbent. Trim the outer edges of the leaves to achieve a solid shape for painting. Then lay your material on a clean, dry surface inside or outdoors, somewhere you can leave it undisturbed.

2. Apply your paint

Apply paint with a paintbrush in the normal fashion. Full coverage is not strictly necessary; allowing the brown to show through in places keeps things looking natural.

3. Leave to dry and repeat

Leave the painted material to dry, then turn it over to paint the other side. If you are using it for a wall hanging or a front-facing arrangement, you might wish to paint just one side.

SPRAYING

You can also add some colour to your dried material with spray paint, which you can buy in small cans from art shops or online. Try spraying delicate fern fronds and distinctively shaped vegetables such as artichokes and see them transform.

1. Prepare your material
As long as it is not windy, it's best to spray outside. Lay your material out on newspaper on a clean, flat surface. Make sure everything is completely dry before you spray: the crispier the material, the better it will hold the paint.

2. Spray and repeat
Spray one colour and one coat at a time with a gentle spritz, and leave to dry. Turn the materials over and repeat. Depending on the look you want to achieve, a second coat may be necessary, but wait until the first coat is dry to the touch. You may not want to fully cover the material in spray paint. Partially sprayed material can also look really stunning: a light coverage allows some of the natural colours to come through and prevents an artificial look.

3. Arrange or store
When you are done, arrange or wrap and store your sprayed material.

Creating a Display

With no need for maintenance or watering, dried flowers can be fashioned and displayed in many different and interesting ways, so just use your imagination and experiment creatively. Discover the joy of styling flowers yourself; make time to create something, and immerse yourself in the 'flow' of doing this. Embrace working with natural elements and notice the effect this has on your sense of well-being.

Treat your dried displays as changeable artworks for blank walls or empty fireplaces, or make small groupings with your favourite possessions on bookshelves or mantelpieces. Create still-life arrangements with other natural finds such as pebbles and shells, driftwood and branches. Follow the principle of 'set and forget', placing your dried flowers in unusual and unexpected places in your home to bring life to dull, dark corners or high-up, out-of-reach spaces. Because they are virtually weightless, they can also be easily suspended from the ceiling or from picture rails to create upside-down displays, so experiment with different heights and lengths.

Be sure to let the flowers do the talking; the stems of dried flowers are rigid and inflexible, so don't try to force them – they'll position themselves naturally if you guide them gently.

Try to restrict the number of different flower varieties you use to prevent a vase arrangement from looking too busy. For large arrangements, create small groupings of the same flower at different heights and angles, and secure them together before adding them to your arrangement.

Forget about creating a perfectly balanced arrangement. Use odd numbers of stems, or go for asymmetrical designs by placing a striking grass or seed head in an off-centre position to draw the eye. A single beautiful stem positioned in the right place has as much visual impact as a whole bunch of flowers. Play around with height and scale: a huge head in a tiny vase, for example, or loose, fluffy bunches in an oversized container. Use monochromatic colour schemes with containers in the same tones and hues as your flowers.

Opposite A repurposed cigar press, handcrafted by JamJar Edit, is a beautifully simple base for a display that emphasizes the different heights of dried flowers and grasses. Test tubes act as supports.

VASES, VESSELS AND BOWLS

When it comes to choosing containers for your dried arrangements, take inspiration from the ancient Japanese philosophy of wabi-sabi. The principles of wabi-sabi are impermanence, simplicity, imperfection, melancholy and asymmetry, and all these elements are present in the process of drying and styling naturally decaying material.

In Japanese culture everything has its own intrinsic value – no single object, whether new or old, is worth more than another. For example, the withering, faded blossoms of the cherry trees or *sakura* are revered just as much as the fresh young buds. Working with dried flowers will teach you to appreciate the perfectly imperfect. Unpretentious arrangements are preferable to anything too contrived or overly ostentatious. This sits well with the modern rustic look of contemporary interiors.

- Look for containers that reflect the sustainable ethos of drying your own flowers – anything that is reclaimed, recycled or repurposed will work well.

- Natural materials already have their own variations and imperfections. Use handcrafted ceramic vessels, earthenware and terracotta bowls, clay pots, hammered metal bowls or carved and chiselled wooden containers to add character and interest to a display.

- Use vases with textured, organic or irregular shapes.

- Avoid anything that looks too new, shiny or mass-produced.

- Trawl charity shops to find inexpensive vintage glassware.

- Don't worry if anything is cracked or chipped: look into *kintsugi* or 'golden joinery', the art of fixing broken pottery with a gold-dusted lacquer. The eye is immediately drawn to the imperfection, but it is made beautiful.

- Buy anything 'new' that looks old – visit craft fairs or find artisan makers who produce small-batch runs of handmade items.

- Start your own collection of vessels in different sizes and shapes, made from the same materials or in the same colours, and you will find that they automatically complement each other when it comes to creating a group display.

KENZAN, FLOWER FROGS AND OTHER SUPPORTS

The thin, wispy stems of dried flowers, grasses and seed pods are not generally strong enough to be self-supporting. There are various ways of helping them to stay upright.

Avoid using dry floral foam, even for a long-lasting arrangement; it is a synthetic, single-use product, and when you eventually want to dispose of it you'll have to send it to landfill, because it doesn't decompose naturally. Instead, try some of these options:

- Scrunch up a piece of chicken wire **(1)** to place inside a bowl or use on a bare surface, arrange your flowers in it and then disguise the wire with soft, dry reindeer moss; it will stay in place if you poke it in gently with a chopstick or skewer.

- Start a collection of kenzan **(2)**, spiky metal Japanese pin holders that come in round or rectangular shapes in various sizes. Place at the bottom of containers to keep stems in place.

- Use old bottles **(3)**, vases with very thin necks **(6)** or shallow containers with extra-narrow openings.

- Make your own grid **(4)** out of firm, dry sticks or stems – rose stems are ideal. Tie or wire them to create small squares for support, and trim to fit across the top of a bowl or shallow container.

- Use dried bushy materials such as gorse **(5)** – the spines will keep your flowers in place – or twiggy balls **(10)**. To mould them into the bottom of a pot, you'll need to soak them so that they are malleable and clump together.

- Intersperse fragile stems with stronger, thicker ones **(7)**, and tie them together before placing them in a vase.

- Look for vintage flower frogs **(8)** and reproduction Victorian-style flower-arranging bowls that have lids with holes in them.

- Make your own holders from balls of craft clay **(9)**: flatten the bottom and make shallow indentations in the top with a pencil. Because dried flowers don't need water, there is no necessity to fire or glaze the clay.

- Improvise with other items that have small holes or openings for inserting dried stems, such as incense stick holders, glass herb pots, salt and pepper pots, and candlesticks.

BASKETS AND WOVEN CONTAINERS

Baskets are having a moment fashion-wise, and are available to buy as handbags in all shapes and sizes and at different prices. When not in use as a fashion accessory, they make brilliant containers for displaying dried flowers, grasses and seed pods. The materials have a natural affinity, and a few loose stems positioned at an angle in a straw handbag hung over the back of a chair look just right, with no complicated, time-consuming arranging tricks required.

- Start a collection of baskets in different weaves and textures.
- Seek out baskets that are handmade or crafted by artisan producers.
- Soft, loose-weave baskets are perfect for filling with a hand-tied bunch, and make a special gift.
- Woven upright containers can be filled with dried material: use a glass bottle or jam jar hidden inside to keep everything standing straight.

- Look for baskets made from reeds, grasses or willow stems, and display dried stems of the same material in the basket for a completely integrated look.
- Attend a willow-weaving or basket-making course to make your own bespoke container; it's immensely satisfying to produce something with your hands, and you'll get a great feel for working with natural materials.

WREATHS

Dried wreaths look fantastic at any time of the year, and are a great way to decorate a blank wall. Swap them around depending on the season and make them in different sizes – starting small if you have only a few materials to hand.

- For any wreath you will need a base. You can make one yourself from dried foraged stems such as willow (*Salix*) or Virginia creeper (*Parthenocissus quinquefolia*).

- You can also buy plain wooden embroidery hoops to use as wreath bases – stain or paint them or keep them natural, depending on your colour scheme.

- Use seasonal colour and ingredients such as berries and mix with long-lasting evergreens such as yew (*Taxus*) and holly (*Ilex*) for a mid-winter festive look. For an autumn harvest theme, try adding seed pods and vegetables such as artichokes.

- To create an environmentally friendly, biodegradable wreath, use natural materials to make the base and secure dry flowers with hemp twine or similar. Then the whole thing can go on the compost heap or to green waste when you have finished with it.

- Hang wreaths on a wall or door, or over a mantelpiece. They also make excellent table centrepieces.

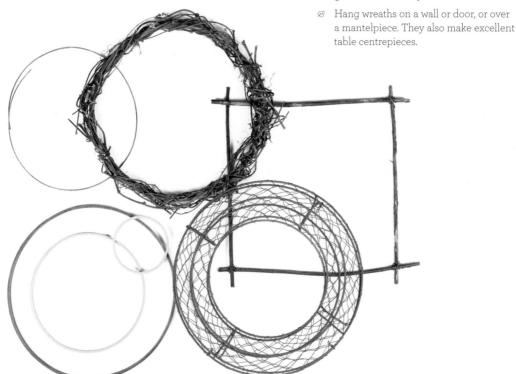

IKEBANA STYLE

Ikebana is the traditional Japanese way of flower-arranging and has been elevated to an art form. It began as long ago as the eighth century, when flowers arranged in a precise style were offered as gifts to the Buddha. Ikebana incorporates both spiritual and philosophical aspects and has evolved into different schools of contemporary practice taught by masters around the world. It takes years to become an accomplished practitioner.

A true ikebana arrangement sits on a kenzan, usually hidden with moss or small stones in a shallow bowl of water, but the principles behind it lend themselves to dried materials:

- Your arrangement should give the illusion of being three-dimensional, even if it is front-facing.

- It should be asymmetric, but keep in mind the shape of a perpendicular triangle and use a single branch or stem to provide line and form to create your top point.

- Follow what happens in nature to create your middle and lower points by using foliage and/or small flowers that would naturally appear at these heights.

- Use materials sparingly and embrace the space in between your flowers. The gaps create harmony.

- Do not be tempted to force your flowers to face in a certain direction. If their undersides are on show, there is a hidden beauty in them that deserves to be revealed.

- Sensitivity to the environment is a fundamental belief.

- Look to the seasons for inspiration.

- Remember that less is always more: it is better to take something away than to keep adding.

- Subtlety, simplicity and even a sense of austerity are the key components, in direct contrast to Western-style flower-arranging, which is all about abundance.

Opposite Ikebana-style dried flower displays with wooden bowls by Elise McLauchlan.

Maintaining Your Displays

When fully dry, your flowers will be wonderfully fuss-free.
Once styled, they can be left well alone for as long as you
like, or you can simply move or swap your arrangements
around to ring the seasonal changes. However you use
your dried displays, you'll want to keep them fresh and
well maintained.

⌀ From time to time, you'll want to refresh
your dried flowers, so just add to them as
necessary and snip out any material that is
looking too tired or jaded.

⌀ If you're living in temporary or rented
accommodation, a dried arrangement is a
quick, sure-fire way of transforming a room
and making an impersonal space feel
like your own. All dried material can be
recycled as green waste, so when you move
out you can dispose of it and start again with
a clear conscience.

⌀ To prevent fluffy grasses from shedding,
give them an all-over spritz with hairspray.

⌀ If flowers start to become too brittle or you
want to display them in a space with heavy
traffic, a coat of spray matt varnish provides
a layer of extra protection. This is a good
way to keep tiny floret-type flower heads
such as hydrangeas intact.

⌀ When you notice that your displays are
starting to get dusty, blow them gently with
a hairdryer on a cool setting or use a soft,
thin paintbrush and a pair of tweezers to
dislodge any sediment.

Projects to Try Yourself

When it comes to designing with dried flowers, there are no hard-and-fast rules – just use whatever materials you have to hand. The ideas suggested over the next pages are easy to re-create and all the ingredients can be substituted. All you really need is a little time and imagination.

HAND-TIED BOUQUET

Bouquets are a wonderful way to bring all sorts of dried material together. Experiment with mixing colours and textures to create different effects. A hand-tied bouquet is a simple place to begin.

Materials:

- Mix of dried foraged grasses, such as moor grass (*Molinia*), Persian rye grass (*Lolium persicum*) and flowering rye grass (*Lolium*)
- Mix of dried foraged flowers, such as brook thistle (*Cirsium rivulare*), ox-eye daisies (*Leucanthemum vulgare*), yarrow (*Achillea*) and rapeseed (*Brassica oleracea*)
- 12 stems of spurge (*Euphorbia*)
- 1 ornamental onion (*Allium*) seed head
- 15 stems of barley (*Hordeum vulgare*)
- Mix of small and large poppy (*Papaver*) seed heads
- 18 stems of greater quaking grass (*Briza maxima*)
- 18 stems of canary grass (*Phalaris canariensis*)
- 3 stems of coneflower (*Echinacea*) seed heads
- 12 stems of love-in-a-mist (*Nigella damascena*) seed pods
- 12 stems of snow-white wood-rush (*Luzula nivea*)
- 3 stems of love-lies-bleeding (*Amaranthus caudatus*)
- Sharp flower snips
- Length of ribbon or twine

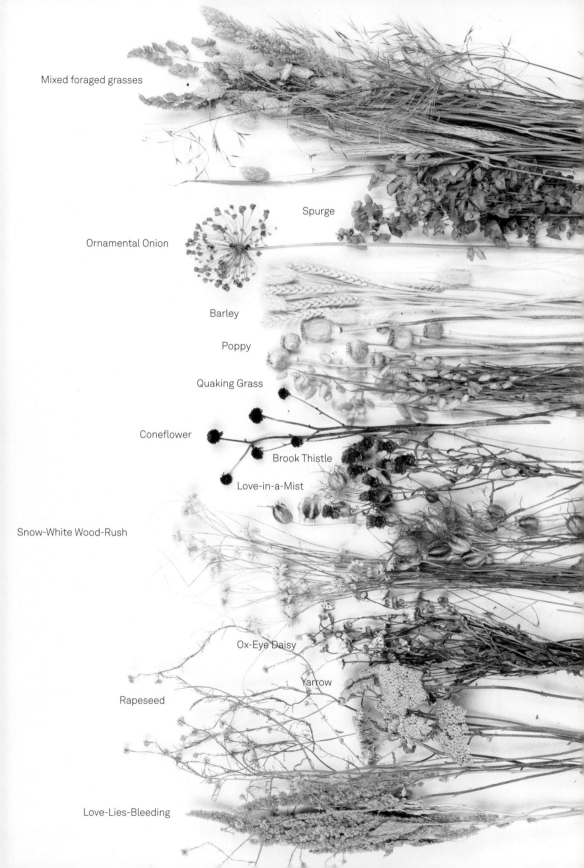

Mixed foraged grasses

Spurge

Ornamental Onion

Barley

Poppy

Quaking Grass

Coneflower

Brook Thistle

Love-in-a-Mist

Snow-White Wood-Rush

Ox-Eye Daisy

Yarrow

Rapeseed

Love-Lies-Bleeding

Step 1

Lay your ingredients in groups on a flat surface in front of you.

Step 2

Start with the single ornamental onion head, or another large round-headed flower, and keep this as your central point. Position the stem between the thumb and forefinger of your left hand if you are right-handed, or your right if you are left-handed. Add a spurge stem to cross over the ornamental onion stem at a slight angle using your other hand. Take hold of it with your first hand and twist clockwise.

Step 3

Gradually add a few stems from each of the plant groups in rotation, twisting in the same direction as you go. You are holding them at what will be the binding point. Loosen your grip and hold midway down the stems for natural-looking results. The higher the binding point, the tighter the bouquet will be.

Step 4
Aim for an even, circular distribution of flowers, grasses and seed heads, and keep checking by holding it up. It's easier to remove anything at this stage than after it is tied.

Step 5
When you are happy with the shape, bind the stems with twine or ribbon using a lasso-style knot. To create a naturalistic look, pull up some of the taller grasses and seed heads so that they tower above the flowers.

Step 6
Finally, cut the stems to the same length on the diagonal. If you plan to display your bouquet immediately in a vase, check the height by holding the bouquet against the vase before you cut anything.

FLAT SHEAF BOUQUET

A flat sheaf bouquet is designed to be front-facing if displayed in a vase, or, to really appreciate it, you can sit it along the length of a mantelpiece or tabletop. Sheaves also work as over-the-arm bouquets and are perfect for brides, lasting long after the wedding celebrations are over. Making a sheaf is easy: it is just a question of layering three or four bunches of dried ingredients, each shorter than the last, and attaching them.

Materials:

- 5 stems of pampas grass (*Cortaderia*)
- 5 stems of bleached oats (*Avena fatua*)
- 10 stems of quaking grass (*Briza media*)
- 10 stems of dyed bunny's tail grass (*Lagurus ovatus*)
- 10 stems of switch grass or cloud grass (*Panicum virgatum*)
- 3 stems of strawflowers (*Xerochrysum*)
- 3 stems of roses (*Rosa*)
- 2 dried magnolia leaves (*Magnolia*)
- 2 trimmed palm leaves (Arecaceae family)
- Twine
- Ribbon
- Sharp flower snips

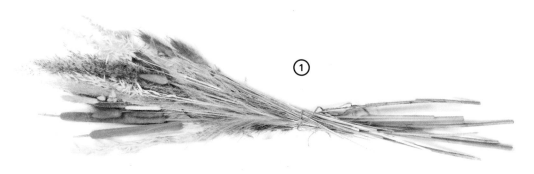

Step 1

Make the first, longest bunch. I have used
a mix of pampas grass, bleached oats and
some quaking grass and bunny's tail grass.
Lay the grasses on a flat surface in a fan shape,
and tie them together at the point where their
stems meet.

Step 2

Make the second bunch, slightly shorter
than the first bunch. Here I have used rose
stems, switch grass or cloud grass, some
shorter stems of quaking grass, and some
strawflowers. Tie them together and fan
out the ingredients gently.

Step 3

For the third bunch, make a small posy of
palm leaves and some more roses. Firmly tie
them together.

Step 4

Finally, lay one bunch on top of the other,
staggering them for a layered effect, and add
a couple of dried magnolia leaves or similar.
Bind tightly with ribbon at the point where all
the stems meet. Trim any long stems so that
you have a neat finish.

WREATH

Wreaths are a wonderful way to combine colours and textures. Forage for grasses, seed pods, berries and whatever is currently available, and weave them together to create a seasonal wall or table decoration.

Materials:

- 10–15 wispy stems of silver birch (*Betula pendula*) catkins
- 16 stems of dried silver grass (*Miscanthus*)
- Assorted dried berries, such as eucalyptus (*Eucalyptus*), and seed pods, such as bladder senna (*Colutea arborescens*) and honesty (*Lunaria annua*)
- 1 stem of sprayed asparagus fern (*Asparagus setaceus*)
- Strong scissors or secateurs
- Florist's reel wire
- 6 stub wires

Silver Birch

Stub Wires

Eucalyptus

Bladder Senna

Silver Grass

Florist's Reel Wire

Honesty

Scissors

Step 1

Make a wreath base from the silver birch
stems by binding them tightly at one end
with a stub wire. Fashion them into a loose
circle about the size of a large dinner plate.
Fix the ends together with another stub wire,
keeping some extra lengths so the catkins
are left to trail.

Step 2

Divide the silver grass into four bunches,
cutting the stems to different lengths. Bind
them with the reel wire and encourage them
to fan out.

Step 3

Attach each bunch to the wreath with the
reel wire, creating a layered effect.

Step 4

Poke the seed head stems through the
bunches of silver grass and some stems of
preserved berries. Position against a plain wall
using a hook or nail.

BIRD'S NEST BASKET

These nests make an elegant
alternative to bases for your
dried flower displays, and
are easily created from vines
or any other woody stems.

Materials:

- 20 or more lengths of old man's beard vine (*Clematis vitalba*), Virginia creeper (*Parthenocissus quinquefolia*), wisteria (*Wisteria*) stems or any other long woody stems pruned from climbing plants

- 1 empty bowl, approximately the size of the basket you intend to make

- Kitchen roll or paper towels

- 3 heavy-gauge stub wires

- Strong secateurs

Step 1
Soak the stems in a large sink or washing-up bowl of warm water for a couple of hours to make them pliable. Shake the water off and wipe them with kitchen roll or a paper towel so they are not dripping.

Step 2
Take 15 or so stems of varying lengths and bind at one end with a stub wire. Starting from your binding point, hold the stems in one hand and loosely wrap them into a round shape over your other hand, using the bowl as a guide to size. Some of the shorter lengths may start to unravel, but you can just poke them back in. When you are happy with the shape, fix the loose ends together with another wire and use the third to secure the whole thing.

Step 3
At this stage you should have what resembles a small, dense wreath. Sit it over the top of the bowl and leave it to dry. You are aiming for an unstructured, organic shape rather than a perfectly round one, but this will ensure that the stems stay together.

Step 4
Use the remaining lengths to create a bottom for your nest. Weave and bind them in a criss-cross fashion to form a flattish layer on which to sit a loose ball of chicken wire.

DISPLAYS UNDER GLASS

Preserving precious dried specimens under glass is a
good way of keeping them dust-free and making them
last even longer.

Domes

Create miniature dried vignettes under glass domes. Use small vases to get tiny bunches of flowers to stand up inside a dome, or use pebbles or a Japanese pin holder (see pages 136–37). Secure them to the base of the dome using double-sided tape. Trim materials to the right height by holding them against the dome before inserting them. Keep your design simple and airy, because once you ease the glass over the top everything will squash together.

Frames

Choose flowers that you have pressed as keepsakes to mount under plain glass frames (see pages 116–19 for pressing instructions). Three or five frames, of the same size or in different sizes, containing various flowers make an interesting display on a plain blank wall, or lined up on a mantelpiece or shelf.

Vessels

Create loose, naturalistic dried arrangements in large glass vases (see page 56). Build up your ingredients from the base using twigs, moss and pebbles before inserting stems of dried flowers and seed heads. Cut the stems to different lengths and place them at angles so that they cross each other for support. For maximum effect, use a series of vases in different sizes and shapes grouped together.

WALL AND DOOR DISPLAYS

Plain white walls and doors are perfect for showing off
seasonal displays of dried stems – it's a quick and easy
way to update your interior decor.

Boards and grids

A metal memo board and some mini wooden
pegs can be used to display favourite dried
flower stems, seed pods and grasses. The
beauty of this display is that it is easy to change
materials and move them about depending
on the season. Use any type of grid for your
display: a piece of wooden trellis would work
as well. Before long stems become too brittle
you can weave them through the gaps and then
use shorter varieties over the top – either poke
them in or use pegs or brass clips – for a multi-
layered effect.

Murals

You can also attach stems of dried and pressed
flowers to a wall or other plain surface to create
a natural mural. Use clear adhesive tape or
Japanese washi tape to add to the decoration.

Envelopes and baskets

Alternatively, fill plain paper envelopes or small
baskets with tiny posies and attach them to a
wall in a pattern of your choosing.

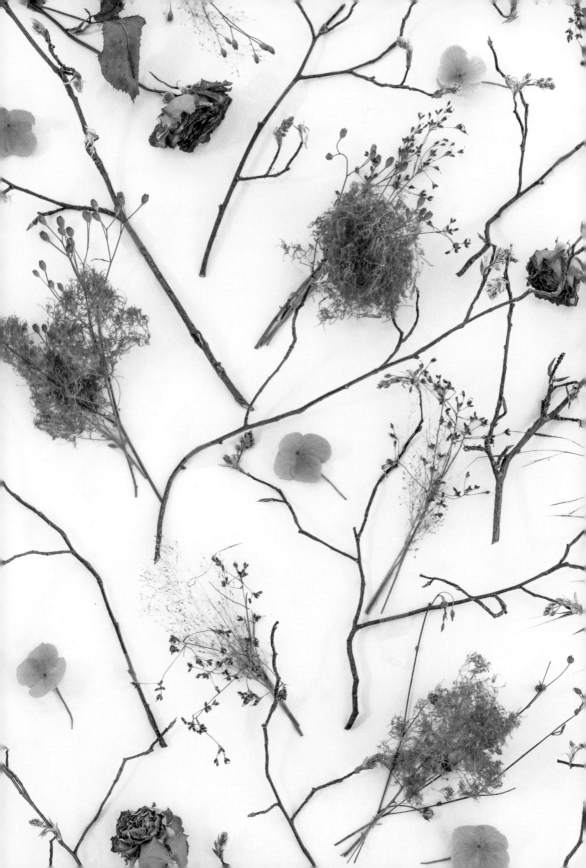

HANGING BRANCH

This is a lovely, natural-looking way of displaying your dried flowers if you have limited materials and space. You can easily swap everything about according to the season, perhaps moving from summer flowers and grasses to autumnal berries and seed pods.

Step 1

Look for branches when you are out walking; a good time to find them is after a storm, when they will have fallen loose from trees. Keep in mind the space where you will be hanging it, so that you can find one to fit.

Step 2

Attach two pieces of twine to the ends of your branch, tying them firmly and leaving the lengths so that you can hang them from hooks.

Step 3

Divide your flowers by type and/or colour and make small bunches of different lengths, securing them with twine and leaving the lengths to tie on to your branch. Lay them out on a flat surface and move them around until you find the order that pleases you most. Attach each bunch to the branch securely, angling the flowers as you do so. Snip off any unwanted ends of twine, and suspend the branch.

Hanging branch display with dried flowers and macrame by Colour & Whimsy.

BOTANICAL CLOUD

Botanical clouds are much easier to make than they look. You can use all manner of ingredients, and they are very light and easy to suspend. I like to see them in groups at different heights and in slightly different sizes floating from the ceiling of a large, airy room.

Asparagus Fern

Materials:

- Various grasses, such as bleached oats (*Avena fatua*), pampas grass (*Cortaderia*), bunny's tail grass (*Lagurus ovatus*) and silver grass (*Miscanthus*)
- Various flowers, such as smoke bush (*Cotinus*) flowers and baby's breath (*Gypsophila*)
- Various seed heads
- Asparagus fern (*Asparagus setaceus*)
- Teasels (*Dipsacus*)
- Transparent nylon thread or fishing wire
- Chicken wire
- Pliers

Smoke Bush

Teasel

Pampas Grass

Bunny's Tail Grass

Baby's Breath

Bleached Oats

Silver Grass

Step 1

Begin by scrunching up a square piece of chicken wire into a loose, organic, cloud-like shape. Attach a length of transparent nylon thread or fishing wire through the top.

Step 2

Push a variety of dried material – long grasses such as pampas and silver grass look great – through the wire so that the ends come out the other side, and snip them off.

Step 3

Start filling the spaces randomly with a mix of other material: sprayed asparagus ferns, teasels, foraged grasses and spiky or round seed heads in neutral tones all complement each other. The idea is to achieve a tactile-looking texture using different shapes that will create an ethereal look while achieving a balanced shape. Fill in any remaining gaps with fluffy dried heads of smoke bush flowers and small bunches of dried baby's breath, or something similar.

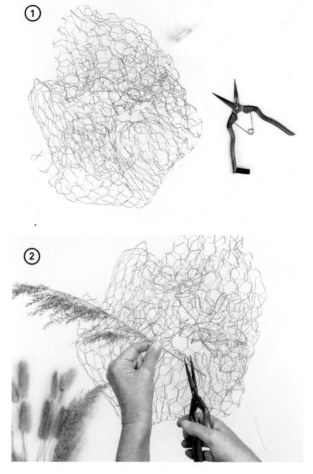

POTPOURRI

Homemade potpourri is the original natural air freshener. Since time immemorial, humans have intuitively and instinctively scattered sweetly scented leaves and flowers around their homes. They disguised unpleasant odours, and certain plants were used to deter insects and were thought to ward off disease. To concoct your own room fragrance from dried material that you have gathered yourself, choose aromatic plants that retain a strong perfume when dried.

Materials:

- Various flowers, such as pansies and violets (*Viola*), chamomile (*Chamaemelum nobile*), roses (*Rosa*), and hibiscus (*Hibiscus*)
- Scented essential oil
- Glass vessel

Step 1
Dry your flowers following the instructions for air drying (see pages 104–6). Try violet and chamomile flower heads, with petals of rose and hibiscus.

Step 2
Once the flowers are dry, mix the tiny violet and chamomile flower heads with the rose and hibiscus petals. You can add a few drops of a scented essential oil to increase the potency.

Step 3
Display in a glass bowl. Mix everything up now and again and refresh with extra drops of essential oil when the scent starts to fade.

Pansy

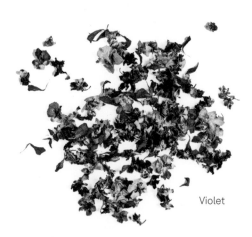

Violet

SMUDGE STICK

Smudge sticks are the new incense. Traditionally, smudging has been practised for centuries by Native American tribes as a way of cleansing the body, mind and spirit. It has been adapted in the twenty-first century as a natural air freshener. Bundles of fragrant herbs around your home will get rid of unpleasant odours. Sage in particular is proven to do this, and has a clean-smelling antiseptic fragrance.

Materials:

- Various fresh herbs, such as sage (*Salvia officinalis*), lavender (*Lavandula*) and rosemary (*Salvia rosmarinus*)
- Cotton thread
- Fireproof dish
- Matches
- Bowl of sand or soil

Step 1

Take fresh clippings of whatever herbs you have to hand. I have used both the leaves and flowers of sage, and some lavender and rosemary stems. Bunch the fresh herbs together with a length of cotton thread before leaving them to air-dry (see pages 104–6). This will take a couple of days. Make sure you tie your ingredients before drying; if you try to tie them afterwards, they tend to break and crumble.

Step 2

Once your herbs are completely dry, it is time to burn your stick and start smudging. This is a ritual to be done with a meaningful intention to clear negative energy and bad vibes. Make sure your room is well ventilated and place your smudge stick on a fireproof dish. Light the end of the smudge stick with a match, and blow the flame out as soon as the stick catches light. The tips of the leaves will start to smoulder and release an aromatic smoke that you can waft around your body and home, inhaling the fresh, perfumed air. It should burn slowly; any ash will collect in the dish.

Step 3

When you have had enough, extinguish your stick by dipping the end into a bowl of sand or soil, so that it is ready for reuse.

Source Directory

Live Plants and Seeds
Chiltern Seeds: *chilternseeds.co.uk*

Crocus: *crocus.co.uk*

Grace Alexander Flowers: *gracealexanderflowers.co.uk*

Higgledy Garden: *higgledygarden.com*

John Cullen Plants (Holders of the National Achillea Collection): *johncullengardens.com*

Knoll Gardens: *knollgardens.co.uk*

Sarah Raven: *sarahraven.com*

Pre-Dried Flowers, Grasses, Foliage and Moss
Atlas Flowers (for buying in volume): *atlasflowers.co.uk*

Daisy Gifts: *daisygifts.co.uk*

The Little Deer: *thelittledeer.co.uk*

Porters Foliage Ltd, New Covent Garden Market: *portersfoliage.com*

Reste: *reste.co.uk*

Triangle Nursery (moss only): *trianglenursery.co.uk*

Urban Outfitters: *urbanoutfitters.com*

Ready-Made Dried Flower Bouquets and Arrangements
Atelier Prairies: *atelierprairies.com*

Botanique Workshop: *botaniqueworkshop.com*

Dot and the Dandelion: *dotandthedandelion.com*

Grace & Thorn ('Some Things Do Last Forever' range): *graceandthorn.com*

Jeanne Paris: *jeanne_paris.com*

The Little Vintage: *thelittlevintage.co.uk*

Pressed Flowers and Pressing Kits
JamJar Edit: *www.jamjaredit.co.uk*

MR Studio London: *mrstudiolondon.co.uk*

Dried Flower Workshops
Grace & Thorn: *graceandthorn.com*

Worm: *weareworm.com*

Vases and Vessels
Elise McLauchlan: *www.mclauchlanmade.com*

Nkuku: *nkuku.com*

Sansho Living (Japanese pots): *sansho.com*

Zuleika Melluish Ceramics: *throwncontemporary.co.uk*

Kenzan and Pin Holders
Chive: chiveuk.com

Graen Studios: *graenstudios.com*

Glass Frames
Nkuku: *nkuku.com*

Botanical Dyed Silk Ribbon
Lancaster and Cornish: *lancasterandcornish.com*

Tools
Nikawi: *nikawi.com*

Acknowledgements

Thank you to everyone involved in the making of this book at Laurence King Publishing, but especially to Zara Larcombe and Jodi Simpson. I think Ida Riveros's images succeed in capturing the hidden, often unseen beauty, in dry or decaying plant material. She draws it to our attention, and I hope this will encourage readers to look again at the cyclical habit of the natural world and consider flowers at all their stages of life with new eyes. Thanks also to Sarah Cuttle, who came not just once but twice on spec to photograph my garden – huge thanks and I'm so glad we have been able to use them.

Once again, my family has borne with me patiently as I have departed on yet another flowery adventure with every available space in our house given over to drying flowers. I'd like to thank them and all the people who have supported me since I decided to follow my instinct and go down the horticultural route twenty years ago. I have been encouraged to pursue my passion, discovering something new and exciting at all the different twists and turns, and this has both challenged and sustained me. I now cannot imagine what else I might have done with my time. For me, whether dry or fresh, home-grown or shop-bought, flowers are a constant – they are for today and forever, and in an uncertain world that brings me comfort and hope.

Photo Credits

All photos are by Ida Riveros, except:

Front and back cover Images by Rita Platts.

Pages 9, 12, and 90 Images by Sarah Cuttle.

Page 48 Image by Graen Studios.

Page 60 iStock.com/Mantonature.

Page 61 Image by Graen Studios. Ceramic vase by Modern Potter.

Page 86 Image by Ida Riveros. Ceramic vase by Karina Smagulova.

Page 118 Image by MR Studio London.

Pages 130 and 163 Images by Nicholas Hodgson.

Page 132 Image by Ida Riveros. Repurposed cigar press kindly loaned by JamJar Edit, with thanks to Redwing PR.

Page 135 Image by Ida Riveros. Handmade cream ceramic pot with embedded *Allium* seed head kindly loaned by Zuleika Melluish @ Thrown Contemporary Gallery.

Page 142 Image by Elise McLauchlan.

Page 165 Image by Colour & Whimsy.

Index